SIX MINUTES IN AUGUST

By Stephen A. Scaffidi

Foreword by Valarie Kaur

SIX MINUTES IN AUGUST

Designed by Christopher Behlmer

For Paramjit Kaur, Satwant Singh Kaleka,
Prakash Singh, Sita Singh, Ranjit Singh and Suveg Singh

Table of Contents

Foreword   i

Introduction   1

Sunday, August 5, 2012   7

Hold for the President of the United States   14

Gurmukh   19

Sunday, August 5th — Evening   25

Learning by Doing: Media 101   31

Gurvinder   38

Meeting Each Other — August 6, 2012   44

National Night Out   49

Lt. Brian Murphy — Six Minutes   71

Sikh Services — Friday, August 10, 2012   76

Meeting the Sikhs   86

One Thousand Paper Cranes   96

Sam Lenda — *"I saw evil in that parking lot"*   116

A Trip to the White House   123

Table of Contents (cont.)

Wade Michael Page	136
Kamal — Losing your Mother	141
How I Got There	145
An Uncommon Bond between Mayors	152
John's Shooting	157
Telling our Story	165
Son of the Temple President	172
The Gun Debate	179
Gurpreet	189
Billings, Montana — Not in Our Town	196
Pardeep and Arno — An Unlikely Alliance	201
Back to the White House	206
SALDEF — Two Years Later	213
A Way Forward	220
Acknowledgments	237
Testimonials	241

Foreword

I first met Mayor Stephen Scaffidi in the haze and clamor that follow a national tragedy. On August 5, 2012, a white supremacist walked into the Sikh Temple of Oak Creek in Wisconsin where people gathered for Sunday morning prayer – and opened fire. He killed six people and wounded many more, including a police officer. It was one of the deadliest hate-based mass shootings in U.S. history.

When I arrived on the scene alongside other Sikh advocates, I witnessed the unspeakable grief of young people who lost their mothers and fathers, aunts and uncles. The massacre would be remembered as the deadliest attack in Sikh American history. But their pain was also tragically familiar: turbans and brown skin have marked Sikh bodies for hate, profiling, discrimination, and violence for more than a century in the U.S., especially since Sept. 11, 2001. The nation's spotlight had never turned to Sikhs long enough to learn our struggles and hopes – until Oak Creek.

Facing the sea of cameras, Sikh Americans, expressed the core principle of the Sikh faith: Oneness. They responded to racial terror with the Sikh spirit of *Chardi Kala* – relentless love and optimism even in suffering. They called for an end to hate, not just against Sikhs but all people.

In response, thousands of fellow Americans gathered in candlelight vigils across the U.S. and sent prayers and letters of support to the victims' families. Though he did not visit, President Obama called the shooting a national tragedy. Flags flew at half-mast and the city of Oak Creek committed its resources to serving the Sikh community.

Leading with humility and strength, always, was Mayor Scaffidi – whose words and actions showed that Oak Creek would not be reduced to the scene of a hate crime but become a beacon of hope. He too embodied the spirit of *Chardi Kala*.

When I sat down with Mayor Scaffidi for an interview in his office that August, he immediately took me to a nearby display case with hundreds of letters from around the world. That outpouring from foreign embassies, governors, and fellow mayors seemed to embolden him. Whatever strength he could muster, he needed it in those days. It's not often a mayor from a small town must manage hundreds of national media requests while an active shooting unfolds. While down the street, families are trying to find answers, the police are still surrounding the scene, and the President calls to offer condolences and the support of the federal government.

Mayor Scaffidi not only managed the moment; he showed that dedicated elected officials could shape the course of history. His police force arrived at the scene in time to prevent additional loss of life, he clearly communicated to the world what had unfolded, and he provided the victims' families unconditional support. Most importantly, he dedicated himself to becoming a friend and ally to the Sikh community, learning our struggles, aspirations, and abiding faith.

I remember when the Sikhs of Oak Creek reentered the *gurdwara* when it was still a crime scene a few days after the shooting. With prayer on their lips, they rolled up their sleeves, ripped out the blood-soaked carpets, and repaired shattered windows, rebuilding their community with their own hands. That weekend, we gathered in the *gurdwara* to pray for the lives of those who were killed, including the soul of the gunman. National media trucks had already left his town, but Mayor Scaffidi remained with the community, sitting with us in the prayer hall, his head covered as is tradition, his hands folded in respect, listening. Since that moment, he has never left our side.

Today, the Mayor serves as a tireless advocate in the movement to combat hate and gun violence in America. He has championed new interfaith partnerships, educational programs, and service organizations such as *Serve2Unite* and *Sikh Healing Collective*. He supported a national campaign calling on the government to change federal hate crimes policy, coordinated by the Sikh Coalition. Sikhs took the fight to Capitol Hill – and won. In early 2015, the government began tracking hate crimes against Sikhs, Hindus, Arabs, and others, for the first time in history, a critical step for violence prevention.

"I'm proud to represent Oak Creek," the Mayor said on the first anniversary of the shooting at the Sikh *gurdwara* in the town he was elected to serve. "Not as a scene of violence, but as a symbol of what one small community can do."

Six Minutes in August is a remarkable chronicle of what happened in Oak Creek through Mayor Scaffidi's eyes. He shows us that the legacy of Oak Creek is not one of bloodshed. It is one of binding wounds, building community, and honoring the best in ourselves and in our country, even when we are faced with its darkest elements.

This book is necessary, now more than ever.

As I write this, the nation mourns the murder of nine black Americans by a white supremacist in Mother Emanuel church in Charleston, South Carolina. As a Sikh American, I am shedding familiar tears. Both Charleston and Oak Creek are part of a long history of racial violence on black and brown bodies in the U.S. But we need not give in to despair.

We must learn from the past.

On the day of the Oak Creek shooting, Lt. Brian Murphy was the first police officer on the scene. He engaged the gunman, took fifteen bullets, and nearly died protecting my people – people who didn't look like him.

"Never let acts of evil usurp the love of God and one

another," Murphy told me after the Charleston shooting. "Be strong, be together, so that one day everyone will be capable of true understanding."

The story of Oak Creek emboldens us to organize a groundswell of action across lines of difference, fortify bonds in our homes and houses of worship, and achieve meaningful change in the halls of power. Oak Creek teaches us how to unwind the coils of fear that restrain us when we encounter those we do not yet know, who may not look like us or pray in the way we pray.

That's why we cannot afford to let Oak Creek fall from national memory. We must hear the story to remember who we are – and honor our heroes and martyrs with action in the present.

When you read *Six Minutes in August*, you become part of the story. You too are charged to carry forth the story of Oak Creek into the world and take action in the spirit of relentless optimism.

Oak Creek and its mayor showed us how to respond to hate and human cruelty, which seek to drive us into despair.

First, we mourn. Then, we organize.

Valarie Kaur, Los Angeles, CA, June 24, 2015

Introduction

"There is shooting (*sound of gunshots*)"

"There is shooting in the building... (*dial tone*)"

These are the words and sounds from the first 911 call that came into the Milwaukee County Sheriff's Department dispatch center shortly after 10:00 a.m. on Sunday, August 5, 2012. It wasn't immediately clear what was unfolding at the Sikh Temple of Wisconsin on Howell Avenue in Oak Creek on that morning, as the dispatcher struggled to decipher the caller's frantic requests to send help, the urgency of the caller's words interspersed with the sounds of gunshots in the background.

As Wade Michael Page, a white supremacist, was methodically moving through the ground floor of the Temple, confronting, and then killing four members inside the building — in addition to the two he had already killed outside — men, women, and children were scrambling to hide, in the basement, and in the pantry, just adjacent to the Temple's kitchen. They had no idea who this man was, or why he intended such violence. They had been praying in the main hall, as they did every Sunday, when their morning was shattered by the arrival of this strange and menacing figure, head shaven, 9mm handgun drawn, who

1

spoke to no one as he moved from room to room, shooting at the members who confronted him. He struggled with and killed Satwant Singh Kaleka, the Temple's president, Prakash Singh, a priest at the Temple, and four other members of the Temple, Sita Singh, Ranjit Singh, Suveg Singh, and Parmjit Kaur, the only woman killed in the attack. He also critically injured Baba Punjab Singh, who was struck in the head by a bullet from Page's gun, and lies in a hospital bed to this day, unable to speak or move on his own.

Page was affiliated with the Hammerskins group, one of the most extreme white-power hate groups in the U.S., with the additional distinction of being a member of several bands linked to the white-power movement, playing at Hammerskins events across the country. Their message was violence and anger towards anyone who opposed their message of white-race supremacy.

On August 5, 2012, none of the members of the Temple knew anything about this group, Wade Michael Page, or why he would want to kill their president or the other members of the Temple. Their immediate concern was getting to safety, and as the day unfolded, finding out who among their members had died. Notifications were slow to come, and many family members did not hear the dreaded news until more than 12 hours after the shooting took place, adding to the grief and shock of an unimaginable day.

The day was filled with chaotic periods of uncertainty. Was there a second shooter? Were hostages taken? Had the shooter escaped? As hundreds of law enforcement officers arrived within an hour of the shooting, from more than 60 different local, state and federal agencies, rumors quickly spread in the community, including among the Temple members, waiting just across the street from the Temple at Classic Lanes. The bowling alley had been taken over by the Federal Bureau of Investigation and local law enforcement. Classic Lanes was typically filled with families enjoying their Sunday afternoons together, but on that day it played host to the surviving members of the Temple, and served as a temporary morgue.

Oak Creek, the city I led as mayor, had never experienced anything like this in our history. We had the occasional homicide, domestic violence incident, and other isolated shootings, but nothing on this scale, nothing with this loss of life and directed at one group, apparently chosen because of how they looked. Our local Sikh Temple of Wisconsin is less than 10 years old, and serves as the place of worship for many Sikh families from around the Milwaukee area. They had been good neighbors, quiet and unassuming. For most of our residents, a neighbor they had never met.

According to the Sikh Coalition website, the Sikh faith is the fifth largest organized religion in the world, with an estimated 25 million members, most of who live in the Punjab area of India. They had in the last century slowly begun to emigrate to the United States, settling mostly in California, the Midwest, and the East Coast. The tenets of their faith — to live honestly, to serve others, to treat everyone equally, and to be generous — were hardly a motivation for any person to target them, but Wade Michael Page had made a connection to this group, and on Sunday, August 5, 2012, he made the conscious decision, apparently aided by his background, including alcoholism and other unknown motivations, to act out.

His actions were quick and systematic. He killed with little acknowledgment of his victims' surroundings. He was there to kill people, and he may have been there to end his own life as well, as quickly as he ended the life of the six members of the Temple. As Murphy arrived on the scene, literally minutes after the shooting started, Page immediately engaged him. He ran directly at him, fired numerous times, and hit Murphy more than a dozen times. The first shot struck Murphy in the throat, damaging his vocal chords. That wound would give Murphy a lasting reminder of that day, each time he speaks.

As Murphy lay bleeding behind a vehicle, Page then

confronted Officer Sam Lenda, the second responding officer on the scene. When Lenda arrived he saw Page, clad in a white t-shirt in the parking lot, initially backing his squad car down the long driveway to assess the situation. Page narrowly missed Lenda with a well-aimed shot to the windshield of the police car, shattering it, Lenda exiting just seconds before the shot. Lenda yelled several times for Page to drop his weapon. When he didn't, Lenda fired a shot into his body, knocking him down. The handgun fell to the ground a few feet away. As Lenda waited for a reaction from Page, he heard a final shot as Page took the handgun, put it to his head, and ended his own life.

From the moment of Murphy's arrival to Page's final shot was a period of just over six minutes. Six minutes of split-second, life or death decisions by two officers, and outstanding police work. Those six minutes ended the incident on August 5, 2012, but the real impact of that day reaches far beyond those directly affected, or even to the families who were devastated by violence and hate. It continues to reverberate in our city and country, the impact of religious persecution, hate crimes and gun violence reaching places as diverse as Aurora, Newtown, Oak Creek and Washington, D.C.

As a newly elected mayor, I was little prepared for any of the events on that day in August. But as our story developed and I met the principal characters in this tragedy — the Temple families, state and federal law enforcement, other elected officials — I am convinced that what happened in Oak Creek could happen again in other places and to other communities — based solely on false perceptions, and an unwillingness to believe in the values of diversity, and a refusal to engage people who look and pray differently than they do.

The story of the city of Oak Creek and the Sikh Temple of Wisconsin is not just one of tragedy based on what happened in August of 2012. It was also the realization, early on, that it could be a starting point for an honest dialogue between a faith-based group who had been ignored, or worse, ridiculed, and the governing agencies charged to protect them. Much of the history of the Sikhs had been written in blood, from their persecution in India, to the attacks on Sikh-Americans after 9/11.

The Sikh Temple shooting once more reminded us that as a nation we have continually failed to address important and far-reaching cultural and societal issues related to civil-rights, violent crime, and justice for all Americans. For a new mayor, it would mean a first year in office spent dealing with the fallout of a mass shooting, but also in a journey of self-discovery and personal development.

Sunday, August 5, 2012

Sunday, August 5, 2012 was a clear, sunny day in Oak Creek, as were most days that summer, at least until mid-morning when my iPhone began to vibrate incessantly, the first of a flurry of texts, e-mails, and phone calls that would quickly put Oak Creek under the glare of an international news spotlight, shining all the way around the world to India.

On the other end of the phone was Fire Chief Tom Rosandich. Tom and I were both sworn into our positions in 2012 and I've known him since our days at Oak Creek High School, and here he was calmly telling me that there was an officer-involved shooting and that he was on his way to the scene. He probably said the words "Sikh Temple" in that conversation, but after I heard the words "officer down," and later read them in a tweet from a local radio reporter, Dan O'Donnell, my anxiety level was quickly rising.

Tom's call was immediately followed up by the same news from Police Chief John Edwards, filling in some of the details, including the identity of the officer, "*Murph*" or Lt. Brian Murphy. He still had very little information on what was happening at the Temple. I had just seen Murphy at an emergency management meeting a few weeks earlier, I remember him joking around in his typical New York style,

7

always in a good mood.

Annie Scholz, then a local television reporter from the NBC television affiliate in Milwaukee, was one of the first journalists on the scene and covered the story throughout the day on August 5, and into the middle of the night. When I later spoke with her about the shooting at the Sikh Temple and her recollections of that day, she remembered getting the call from her assignment editor during the middle of a run, hurriedly changing and driving down from Milwaukee to Oak Creek with her photojournalist.

They arrived quickly enough to find a spot for their satellite truck in the crowded, chaotic parking lot of Classic Lanes and immediately began gathering video from the family members. Many were still streaming out of the Temple, or just arriving on-scene, frantically trying to find out what had happened. The family members she spoke with had very little information at that time, and Scholz remembered letting small groups of four or five into their satellite truck to watch local and national coverage of the shooting. "They were in shock and just listening, sitting there in this crowded truck with us watching the video monitors, trying to find out anything they could," Scholz recalled.

With more than 10 years of experience as a television reporter, Scholz noted that many calls she was sent to by her assignment desk never turned out to be significant. In this case, it was the opposite. "This was so much worse, and seeing the people and family members milling around the parking lot made me realize this was very different," Scholz said. "The networks began to show up, and I was getting calls from CNN," she said. "The parking lot was quickly filling up with law enforcement and vehicles, and I could just tell that this was a much bigger story than anything else I had ever covered."

As I drove to City Hall, my mind was racing. Was Murphy OK? How many killed or injured? Any other officers hurt? Why Oak Creek? I did not know it then, but it would be many hours before any of these questions were answered, and one of them may never be.

Oak Creek is a city of 35,000 people, just south of General Mitchell International airport, on the southern edge of Milwaukee County, bounded by Lake Michigan on the east, and sharing a border with the City of Franklin along South 27th Street, the old, historic US Highway 41. It is one of the fastest growing cities in Wisconsin, transitioning from a rural past to a more modern, diverse future. In April, I had been sworn in as the ninth mayor in the history of the City of Oak Creek, after serving two terms as an alderman. I became the new part-time mayor leading a city that had spent most of the last year debating whether to create a new downtown on the site of an old General

Motors plant.

On the first Sunday in August, I was now thrust into the role of spokesperson for a city that had just suffered one of the most horrific acts of violence in the history of our country, in a place of worship filled with members of the Sikh faith, and I would be doing it at a news conference shown live on television in almost every country on earth. Later in the week, a relative who was on a trip to Italy told me they heard my voice first, then looked at the CNN live feed, and noticed that it was Oak Creek, Wisconsin on the bottom of the screen. For the next two hours, they sat in a hotel room in Florence, Italy, watching the events of August 5 unfold.

Directly across the street from the Sikh Temple of Wisconsin is Classic Lanes, a decades-old bowling center on Howell Avenue, the main north-south thoroughfare in the city. In the hours following the shooting at the Temple, their parking lot would play host to 400 law enforcement officers from the Bureau of Alcohol, Tobacco and Firearms, FBI, and personnel from local police and fire departments responding with mutual aid. The building served as a temporary morgue, interviewing location and family assistance center.

When I arrived on scene, it seemed surreal: armored vehicles, tactical command centers, and dozens of officers rapidly donning vests and SWAT gear. My first thought: I've only ever seen this in movies. *DieHard* came to mind. I could not believe this was happening here. When they asked me to move back, I listened. A safety vest was quickly handed to me, and I put it on, not that it made me feel any safer. The scene was still fluid, questions swirling: Were there any other shooters, any hostages in the building, how many victims?

By noon, most of the city leadership had been notified, and the City Administrator and City Attorney had arrived on scene. At that point, there wasn't a ton I could do out there, other than to support my two chiefs and begin the process of putting together a public statement. In my first four months on the job, I had not even written a press release, let alone held a press conference. I thought about what I would say, what the message would be. The words "tragedy, victims, thoughts and prayers," ran through my mind. Oak Creek's City Attorney Larry Haskin began putting some thoughts down on paper; my handwriting is almost illegible, so that was an easy choice. As we sat in one of the command center trailers just across the street from the Sikh Temple, City Attorney Haskin and I crafted a brief official statement from the city, one I would read later at the first official press conference at 4:00 p.m. Central time that day, standing just to the east of the Temple, across Howell Avenue, directly in front of a former United Auto Workers Union building.

The City is outraged by this senseless act of violence that occurred in our city today. We extend our sympathies to the families of the victims. Our thoughts and prayers are with them. We are grateful for the heroic actions of our officers. As it has been reported, one of our officers has been shot and wounded. Please join me in praying for his recovery. The City of Oak Creek will cooperate with all federal, state, and county officials as this investigation continues.

Police Chief John Edwards was also newly sworn in to his leadership position, but his tenure on the Oak Creek Police Department was significant, having served in the department for more than 25 years. John wasn't just my police chief; he is also one of my closest friends. The fact that we had known each other for decades certainly made our shared responsibilities in the aftermath of the shooting easier to manage. He also had a direct connection with officer-involved shootings; he had been a victim himself, at the very beginning of his career.

As I stood outside on the asphalt parking lot of Classic Lanes, on what was turning into a very warm day, I noticed that I was getting repeated calls from a number that showed up as *blocked* on my iPhone. At that point, I had been ignoring almost every call, unless it was from city staff, or someone I recognized from the fire or police

12

departments. This had gone on for at least an hour when I saw Tom (Chief Rosandich) run up to me, saying (as best I can remember), "Answer your phone. Someone from the White House is trying to get a hold of you. Next time you see a *blocked* call, answer it." In the next half hour, my phone rang again, and Tom was right. *Blocked* showed up on my screen, and it was the White House, informing me that I would receive a call from a high-ranking government official in the next hour. If I didn't realize it before, Oak Creek was in the national news and on everyone's mind, including someone calling from Washington, D.C.

Hold for the President of the United States

I was sitting in my car just outside the east entrance of City Hall when my phone rang again, displaying a now familiar *blocked* on my iPhone screen. I had left the parking lot of Classic Lanes a few moments earlier, just after the late-afternoon press conference, to return a few phone calls from my office at City Hall and pulled into a parking spot adjacent to the building. Forewarned that a call from a "high ranking government official" was coming, I did not hesitate to answer it.

When Irene Hsu, from the Office of the Press Secretary of the White House, asked me to identify myself, I quickly complied. The next words she said nearly sucked the air out of my lungs, "Hold for the President of the United States." As a mayor, you get used to talking to other elected officials regularly. Wisconsin Governor Scott Walker had visited Oak Creek many times, as recently as May of 2012, and Congressman Paul Ryan and U. S. Senator Herb Kohl had also visited our city during my time in office. However, as a mayor of a city of 35,000 people, on the job for less than four months, I was fairly certain I would not be interacting with the leader of the free world at any point during my term. That had all changed now.

As the President began to speak, I sat up stiffly in the front seat of my car, holding the phone as close to my ear as

possible, listening to a familiar voice, familiar only from
hearing it a thousand times on television, as the
presidential election campaign had recently begun to heat
up. I thought about how odd it seemed that a conversation
of this importance would be taking place between the
White House and the front seat of my blue 2005 Ford
Escape parked next to an Oak Creek municipal building,
significantly smaller and less relevant than the one in
Washington, but at the center of the universe in today's
news.

Many people have asked me about the call from President
Obama and to be honest, he really was exactly as you
would expect a President to be. His voice was calming,
slow and reassuring; presidential, I guess. The President
promised the full support of the federal government, a
promise he kept, and offered his family's thoughts and
prayers for the Temple shooting victims families and to our
community. I'm sure I expressed my thanks for his kind
words, but in the moment, I probably did more listening
than talking. In the months after the shooting, I've talked
about that call and its significance to me in calming my
anxiety and reducing my stress levels, which had climbed
throughout the day. The President did what the President
should do in times of crisis: tell us everything will be all
right, and we'll all get through this together. In January of
2013 I had the chance to travel to Washington, D.C., and in
a small room adjacent to the East Room of the White

House, I thanked him for that call in person. He was just as gracious then as he was in August.

In the late afternoon of August 5, the White House released a statement by the President on the shooting which read:

> *Michelle and I were deeply saddened to learn of the shooting that tragically took so many lives in Wisconsin. At this difficult time, the people of Oak Creek must know that the American people have them in their thoughts and prayers, and our hearts go out to the families and friends of those who were killed and wounded. My Administration will provide whatever support is necessary to the officials who are responding to this tragic shooting and moving forward with an investigation. As we mourn this loss which took place at a house of worship, we are reminded how much our country has been enriched by Sikhs, who are a part of the broader American family.*

Reading these words now, I'm struck by the fact that my life has also been enriched by the Sikh community, a group who I knew very little of before the shooting. As an elected official, my only interaction with any members of the local Sikh Temple of Wisconsin was in a Common Council meeting early in my political career, as Aldermen in the 3rd

16

District of Oak Creek. Having spent many hours inside the
Temple, or *gurdwara,* since the shooting, I've learned
many of the customs and tenets of their faith. One of their
principal beliefs centers on equality, that all human beings
are equal, and perhaps more importantly are welcome
inside their house of worship. Since August 5, I have been
invited into the Temple on many Sunday afternoons to
celebrate with the Sikh community. On Sunday, November
11, 2012, I was given the highest honor of the Sikh faith,
when I, along with Police Chief John Edwards, was
bestowed with saffron-colored robes of honor, or *siropas*,
at a ceremony in front of the entire Temple community,
for our *seva*, or service after the shooting.

Each time I visit, I'm touched by the kindness and the
compassion of its members. Gurvinder Singh is a high
school age Sikh who arrived in the United States after his
father Ranjit Singh lost his life in the August 5 shooting.
Kanwardeep Kaleka, nephew of the slain Temple President
Satwant Singh Kaleka, is a PhD candidate and a youth
educator at the Temple who speaks so eloquently and
thoughtfully on the subject of non-violence, despite the
bloody brutality of the rampage within the Temple where
he worships. All of the members, from very young to very
old, hold on to their core belief that despite what
happened, and more specifically, where it happened, they
would hold their community together, and expand that
definition of community to include Oak Creek and beyond.

I've said many times since August of 2012 that the realities of that day, and the personal experiences that resulted from it, were life changing. As I think back to that three minute phone call with the President of the United States, on a day which seemed like any other summer day until Wade Michael Page ended the lives of six people, and his own, my mayor's job had now taken on a different role. From that day forward, being mayor meant more than balancing the budget and running the city meetings. I was now tasked with trying to make sure that Oak Creek was known for our response to the events of August 5 and not as one more city in a long line of cities known primarily for mass shootings. The list is long; Columbine, Tucson, Blacksburg, Aurora and Newtown, each with its own story of violence, each with a unique twist on how that violence manifested. Ours was inspired by evil and hate, fueled by an assumption based on nothing more than a turban, and faces that looked somewhat different from the rest.

Gurmukh

Shortly after 10:00 a.m. on the morning of August 5, 2012, Gurmukh Mangat was at the Wisconsin Athletic Club, a fitness club where he worked out regularly. A friend who ran up to him, his mouth wide open, shouting "someone shot up the Temple," interrupted his bench press routine. Stunned, Gurmukh immediately thought of his father, who had told him earlier that he was going to stop by the Sikh Temple of Wisconsin later that morning. His friend had glanced at his phone and noticed a flurry of Temple-related texts and social media posts, many of which were saying that someone was shooting inside the Temple, and that as many as 25 people had been killed.

Gurmukh, the son of a gas station and convenience store owner in nearby Madison, Wisconsin, was a Sikh, having been baptized into the religion as a young man growing up in Windsor, Ontario, Canada. Early in his life he learned to play the *tabla*, the drums used to accompany the singers in his local *gurdwara*.

When he was 16, his family moved to Madison, a move that he struggled with early in his life. His turban and beard set him apart from his classmates at a predominately white high school in McFarland, Wisconsin, just outside Madison. To the dismay of his father, he cut his long hair and beard, a decision many young Sikhs in the

United States and elsewhere face, their faith meeting American culture head-on.

He hurriedly jumped in his friend's car, and began calling to find out where his father was, quickly discovering that he was safe at a nearby *gurdwara* in Brookfield, Wisconsin. Despite that knowledge, the fear that something significant and terrifying was happening in Oak Creek to friends and members of his own faith caused him to double over, his body shaking hard, sobbing loudly and uncontrollably, crying harder than he had cried in a long time. As he struggled with his emotions, he drove toward Oak Creek, hearing the worst from members inside the Temple, and from family and friends beginning to understand the scale of the terror inside.

Getting near the Temple was not going to be easy. Law enforcement had already sealed off the area, limiting traffic on surrounding streets and questioning anyone who was moving within the perimeter set up around the Temple. As he approached the scene, he was able to park fairly close, only a few blocks away, and approached a news van, which had already set up a satellite truck nearby. Identifying himself as a member of the Sikh faith, and someone who could speak both English and *Punjabi*, the reporter quickly realized that he was an asset and asked him several questions about the Temple and whether or not he knew anyone inside.

Talking to Gurmukh more than a year after the shooting, it was still clear in his descriptions of that morning that the fear and the uncertainty he felt in the first few hours were significant, but those fears also drove him to want to be there and to help in any way he could, pushing him to try to get as close as possible, despite hundreds of law enforcement personnel trying to keep him out.

Wanting to do something to contribute, he purchased three cases of bottled water from a local grocery store and handed them out to anyone who needed one, eventually meeting up with the local Salvation Army volunteers, who were also immediately on the scene, handing out both water and sandwiches. As the day went on he served multiple roles, as an interpreter between the non-English speaking Temple members and law enforcement, and as an unofficial grief counselor and volunteer for the Temple families, many of who still had no idea who was injured, or worse, dead. The nearby Brookfield *gurdwara* delivered a *langar* meal directly from their Temple, traditionally a vegetarian meal served in a *gurdwara* for anyone who wishes to eat. Trying to instill some normalcy into a day filled with uncertainty, Gurmukh helped feed the Temple families from the large food buckets, as he had done on many Sundays before.

As the day went on, Gurmukh and other family members consoled and helped each other cope with the shock, anxiously waiting for the official notifications of who had been killed or injured. Later in the evening Gurmukh recalled seeing Kamal Saini, a teen-aged member of the Temple, walking with his head down across the parking lot of Classic Lanes, the bowling alley directly across the street from the Temple. As someone asked him what was wrong, Kamal fell to the ground in complete agony, a son who had just been told that his young mother, Paramjit Kaur, only 41 years old, had been killed in the Temple, and that he would never see her alive again.

Hour after hour, scenes of incredible compassion and utter disbelief continued inside the bowling alley, and outside, as family members learned who was killed, and relatives and friends came to offer their assistance. Gurmukh spent that day helping others, a key tenet of his Sikh faith that despite his decision to cut his hair and beard had stayed strong throughout his life. As the evening came, and families struggled to accept the news of the incredible loss of life, he served his Temple family, offering help wherever he could.

The area around the Temple and Classic Lanes would serve as the center point of local and national attention for many days after the shooting. It was a place of enormous sadness and grief, stretching the physical boundaries of the Temple across the street, hosting not only the families of the victims, but also the many law enforcement agencies on the scene, who were investigating the crime scene, and providing security. Howell Avenue remained closed for several days after the shooting, making it easier for the police officers and Federal agents to move freely, but remaining as a barrier to the Temple families, who were not allowed to return to the Temple until later in the week.

Gurmukh, who has asthma, said one of his clearest memories from that day is the kindness of an Oak Creek resident, who, when he told them he was having trouble breathing, arranged to get him an inhaler, "saving his life," as he later put it. He had forgotten to bring one with him, and on top of all the chaos of that day, his physical needs were challenging his own ability to provide assistance to others. He remained at Classic Lanes until late into the evening, eventually collapsing on his bed, his emotions and physical strength tapped from a day spent dealing with something he never thought would happen to his family and to members of his own faith.

With a degree in Finance from the University of Wisconsin—Madison, Gurmukh still spends a significant amount of time with his father's business interests, but music also continues to be a big part of his life. In the days after the shooting, his ability to understand how best to present the Sikh faith in a positive, relatable manner would go a long way in helping our residents cope with the tragedy. His willingness to get involved, to educate, and to help heal, were instrumental in the story of the first week after August 5, and his efforts would help Oak Creek take its first few shaky steps forward after the shock of Sunday slowly began to wear off.

Sunday, August 5th — Evening

Late in the day on August 5, we had convened a hastily arranged administration meeting to assess where we were, and what the next few days might look like from a logistics perspective. City Attorney Larry Haskin, City Administrator Jerry Peterson, and Public Information Officer Doug Seymour, who typically serves as the Director of Community Development for Oak Creek, joined myself and a few other members of the City Hall staff in a small office on the east side of the City Hall Building. At this point, we were still being bombarded with media requests, and Seymour had essentially given the same message to all of them. "The Mayor and the Police Chief will be available tomorrow morning at the Oak Creek Police Department beginning at 5:00 a.m." We knew the networks were setting up as early as 4:00 a.m. because many of them had contacted our PIO about where the next day's press conference would be held.

We had stuck to the "no additional comments for today" mantra since the first press conference was held just across the street from the Sikh Temple in the late afternoon, but I had agreed to do one interview later in the evening from my home. A British Broadcasting Company producer in England had reached out to me by email and phone and in a moment of weakness, or maybe a nod to the country of my birth, I agreed to do an interview with the BBC around 10:00 p.m. Central Daylight time, or very early in the morning in London. I was born in an Air Force Hospital in Burderop Park, England in 1958. My father Dominic, who was stationed there in the late 1950s, met my mother Agnes on a blind date at Big Ben. My mother, born in England, who lived with her mother and grandmother in Oxford, tells the story that each of them were waiting at different locations around the iconic London landmark, and after a half hour or so of waiting, each started walking back, believing they had been stood up. At some point, they ran into each other, and their history, and mine, was set on its course.

As I left City Hall, and drove the few blocks to my house, I thought about the last 10 hours, and what they meant for my city and our future, hoping that Murphy would be OK, and that the injured members of the Sikh Temple would not only survive but recover from their injuries. I wasn't home for long, just enough time to splash some cold water on my freshly-sunburned face, as I was soon heading to Froedtert Hospital with my wife Kathy, who had watched all of the day's events unfold on local and national television at our home.

Murphy was still undergoing surgery on his damaged throat into the evening, and both Police Chief John Edwards and I wanted to make sure that we stopped at the hospital that night to check on his condition. We also wanted to add our presence to the growing show of support in the waiting room on the second floor. When we arrived at Froedtert, we were hurriedly escorted up by the hospital security, and as we approached the waiting room, we saw many of our own Oak Creek police officers, and members of Murphy's family, sitting and standing in the small area just off the hallway leading to the ICU. His wife Ann was seated, and as I knelt next to her chair and offered her my family's support and prayers, I could sense the raw emotion and uncertainty about her husband's condition in her eyes. Brian and Ann had only been married for a short time, and although any police officer's spouse is surely aware of the dangers of the job, I doubt this was in her mind when he went off to work on that Sunday morning.

I later learned that Murphy was actually scheduled to be off that morning, but had covered for a co-worker who needed the day off. In the ultimate version of *Murphy's Law,* he had been shot in the line of duty, and was now lying in an operating room, surgeons working to repair more than a dozen bullet wounds to his body.

The surgeon who had been working on his throat, Dr. Travis Webb, came out and spoke to Chief Edwards and me at some point, explaining that much of the surgery was related to his trachea and vocal chords, which were heavily damaged in the shot which had traveled through the side of his neck and exited to the front. The tone of the conversation at that point was actually very optimistic: none of the wounds appeared to be life threatening, and most of the delicate work being done on his throat was meant to improve his speaking abilities once he recovered. As Murphy recovers to this day, many months later, his voice is still rough and raspy, a permanent wound to his physical body, but not limiting enough to halt his incredible spirit and the Brooklyn-ese style of speaking he carries with him from his days growing up in New York.

I was touched by the show of support from many of the other first-responding officers from that morning, who worked long hours at the crime scene, but still had found the energy to be with Murphy and his family this night. The officers sat quietly with his wife, many of them still in uniform from the day, offering a show of solidarity and camaraderie familiar to those in the law enforcement community, and something I became aware of in my short tenure as Mayor. In my official role, I attended swearing-in and commendation ceremonies at the police station on a regular basis, and admired the highly respected and well-trained Oak Creek police department. The show of strength and community at the hospital didn't come as any surprise.

We drove home quietly. At this point, I hadn't eaten anything since early this morning, and I was beginning to feel the weight of the day, my body reminding me that that at some point, regular programming needed to resume. As I stepped into my house, which now felt somehow foreign and not quite right, I sat down in a chair in my living room, and closed my eyes for a few moments, rubbing my forehead as I slowly sunk into the chair. At some point, I turned on the television and was instantly reminded of the day's events, this time from a media perspective, learning details about the shooter that I hadn't picked up, even as I stood all day across the street from the Sikh Temple. Wade Michael Page, who was living in a nearby city with his girlfriend until that morning, had killed six people and wounded several others, in the city that I led as Mayor. An odd thing to hear, even after having spent the day living it.

After eating some warmed-up dinner, I contacted both sets of parents, reassuring them that I was OK (as far as I know, sunburn wasn't life threatening), filling in some of the details, at least what I was able to tell them at that point in time. I walked into my home office just before 10:00 p.m., sat in my chair, and waited for the call from the BBC producer, wondering what I would say, what I should say, and whether or not I was ready to do an interview which would be broadcast across an entire country several thousand miles away. I jumped when my iPhone began vibrating suddenly. I had forgotten to switch it back to ring tone. It startled me, and caused a momentary state of panic as the BBC producer greeted me on the other end of the line, running through some quick audio checks and outlining the questions he would ask me. I was back in my homeland; at least my voice was, 53 years later, talking to a country home to a large population of Sikhs, many of who were in a state of shock just as real as it felt here in Oak Creek. For the Sikh community, August 5 was a day of harsh realities and unfathomable pain. Their faith had been challenged, not by a country, but by an individual, who may have not even bothered to know the real identity of the group he thought he was targeting.

As the interviewer asked me about the shooting, the injuries to Murphy and the other details of the day, I felt even more drained. It had been a day of unimaginable horror and sadness played out in our community. It would take time and a great deal of support to recover from that, with just a few hours before the spotlight would be turned on again.

Learning by Doing: Media 101

There is probably nothing more terrifying for the average person than having a microphone thrust in your face on live television, and being asked about something before you've had a chance to comb your hair, straighten your collar, or even formulate an opinion in your own mind. That's usually a recipe for embarrassment, or worse yet, a chance to say something you'll later regret.

As an elected official, the situation becomes even more critical when it involves serious subject matter, and in the case of the Sikh Temple of Wisconsin shooting, with international interest, and on the heels of the recent mass shooting in Aurora, Colorado, I was now certainly on center-stage. I had never been interviewed before on local or national television, although I had asked a question from the audience on an episode of the Phil Donahue show in Chicago in the early 1980s, on a show having something to do with Brown University and a suicide pill, if my memory serves me.

Part of the conversation between Chief John Edwards, our PIO Doug Seymour, and myself late in the day on August 5 focused on the rapidly growing list of media requests for interviews, and how we would approach them. It was decided fairly early on that we would let the afternoon press conference speak for itself, and pretty much stay off television until after the Monday morning 10:00 a.m. police department press conference, giving us a chance to catch our breath, and for the details of the incident to be become a little clearer. Whatever time I had between that decision and 5:00 a.m., when the network interviews started, I would need a plan. At that moment, we knew seven people were dead, including the shooter Wade Michael Page, and three others injured, but the specifics of that morning were still a long way from being known. In addition, I certainly wasn't ready to say much more than what was already out there.

On Sunday evening while I was in City Hall, I received a phone call from Aurora, Colorado Mayor Steve Hogan. He had just lived through the experience of a mass shooting two weeks earlier, a gunman killing 12 people at a midnight screening of the film *The Dark Knight Rises*. Mayor Hogan, who had been elected to office in 2011, expressed his personal condolences for what happened and those of his city, still grieving from their own mass shooting. He also offered some guidance and I still remember the words he used: "talk about what you know." He advised me to stay away from speculation and to let the residents know that things would be all right. Hogan's willingness to share his direct experience and the pain of what he had just gone through was critical to my early response and strategies with the public and the media.

I thought about that advice as I lay in bed late Sunday
night, and early Monday morning, and made a conscious
decision to keep my comments brief, focusing on our
community's expression of grief for the victims and their
families and our wounded officer, Lt. Brian Murphy. I also
wanted to reassure our residents of their safety. Months
later, I had the chance to talk with Mayor Hogan in
Washington D.C. and personally thank him for reaching
out to me, a new mayor, also dealing with an act of
violence in a city unaccustomed to acts of hate carried out
in such a brutal, senseless manner. Aurora has over
300,000 residents within its borders; Oak Creek has just
fewer than 35,000. Two cities, separated by more than
1,000 miles, but both reeling from horrific mass shootings,
one in a movie theater, one in a temple, but both inflicted
on people who never saw it coming.

As Monday morning arrived, I put on my dark blue suit, the
same suit I had worn in 2009 when I was honored with
Oak Creek's Citizen of the Year award, and began the short
drive over to the Oak Creek Police Station on Ryan road,
just a few miles from my house. As I drove down Howell
Avenue, I thought about what this day would look like. I'd
certainly seen enough of these press conferences to know
how they go, and I was determined to put our city in the
best possible light and not do anything to take the
attention away from the fact that six people had been
brutally killed by a white supremacist in their house of

worship on a quiet, Sunday morning in Wisconsin.

For whatever reason, as I was writing my statement the night before, the phrase "do not let this tragic event define us" was swirling inside my head, and it began to take shape as a way of consciously moving us away from being known only as one of those cities that has seen senseless violence, to a city known more for its response to tragedy. This was something that made sense to me early on, and I've carried that theme along with me in speeches, interviews, and many other public forums since then.

If my view of the command center across the street from the Temple had reminded me of a scene from a Bruce Willis movie, then my first take on the sea of TV satellite trucks that were lined up in front of the Oak Creek Police Station were also reminiscent of every movie media scene I had ever seen. Nearly every major national network and many of the local affiliates from Chicago, Milwaukee, and Madison were in place to begin the process of covering the story. The sea of equipment spread across the small drive and parking lot of the police station was more than enough to grab my attention as I drove in.

Each of the networks had set up their equipment on the circle drive in front of the station, or inside in the courtroom, which had now become a maze of cameras, light stands and wires. The police station was the newest of our city buildings, and could easily handle the crush of the media, but its technological limits certainly were being tested. *Good Morning America* was first up at 5:00 a.m., and Chief Edwards and I were ushered into the courtroom. The camera crew quickly applied some makeup to cover the deep red sunburns we had acquired yesterday after spending the entire day Sunday outside in the hot sun. As we typically did in our conversations, we lightened the mood by joking about the makeup application, and how a week earlier we had been sitting in a lake in northern Wisconsin, sharing beers and jokes, with some of our old high school friends. When you've known someone as long as John and I have known each other, it was easy to provide the support and encouragement we would need in the coming days and weeks.

We quickly made the round of network interviews and a few with the local stations before assembling in the judge's chambers immediately adjacent to the courtroom. Doug Seymour introduced Teresa Carlson, Special Agent in Charge of the Milwaukee Office of the Federal Bureau of Investigation, James Santelle, U.S. Attorney for Southeastern Wisconsin, Chief Edwards, and myself. We would be speaking in front of a packed courtroom, which included not only members of the media, but also at least a dozen members of the Sikh Temple seated in the first row.

Just before I stepped up to the microphone to read a brief statement about Sunday's events, John ran me through what he needed from me this morning. I listened and said, "I got this," and walked up to the microphone. As I stood there facing the audience, I put on my reading glasses, still needing them to read from my two pages of prepared text, which I had deliberately oversized to avoid having to put on my glasses. My mouth dry from nervousness, I spoke quietly but forcefully, calming myself as I said the words that I thought our community needed to hear, offering my prayers and support to the families of the victims, and to Murphy and his family, who were coping with his significant injuries in a hospital, a half hour away from where we stood.

Here is the text of my comments during the Press Conference on August 6, 2012, delivered in the courtroom at the Oak Creek Police Department:

> *Sunday was a tragic day for our city, especially given the fact that it occurred in a place of worship, at a Sunday service, on a quiet Sunday morning in Wisconsin. Our thoughts and prayers go out to the families of the victims, for our wounded officer, all our responders, fire, police, and other agencies, and the community, which is still in shock.*

> *There is no doubt in my mind that the heroic*

*actions of our officers prevented an even greater
tragedy, and they should be commended for that.
Oak Creek is a diverse, welcoming city. We host
twenty-three places of worship and the Sikh
community is part of that . . . what makes our city
strong. We will recover from this, but I want to
assure everyone that we are doing everything we
can, cooperating with federal, local and state
agencies, to get the answers we need to resolve the
situation, and to begin the healing process.*

*As part of that, we will have a community-wide vigil
as part of our National Night Out event tomorrow
night at 8:30 p.m., adjacent to the Oak Creek
Community Center on Howell Avenue.*

Looking back on that morning now, less than 24 hours
after one of the most vicious attacks in our country's
history, I remember a sea of faces and cameras filling the
room, each there to tell the story of the shooting, each
with a different perspective on what it might mean, or
how this could happen here in a small city like Oak Creek,
unaccustomed to violence and hate crimes.

Gurvinder

Gurvinder Singh was just 15 years old and had never been to the United States when he got a call, late in the evening on Sunday night, August 5, 2012, from his uncle in New Jersey, telling him that his father had been killed in the shooting at the Oak Creek *gurdwara*. Gurvinder, or *Guru*, as he likes to be called, had talked with his father on the phone almost daily since he had left India to go to work in the United States, but he had only seen him through photographs, since his father had left India in 1997. Only seven months old when his father moved to the United States, tragically Guru's first trip to America brought him to Oak Creek to attend his father's funeral services on the Friday after the shooting. His family, traveling to America not to celebrate a new life together, but to mourn the loss of their father and husband.

Guru has two sisters, both married, and moved in with his mother close by the Temple, where his father had lived and worked. In the weeks and months after the shooting when I would visit with him, he was still reeling from the news that he would never reunite with his father, angry and struggling to help his mother cope with the loss.

His father, Ranjit Singh, had served as a priest at the Sikh Temple of Wisconsin and had been planning a visit back to India in October of 2012 to see his now teenage son, and to celebrate the Indian Festival of Lights, or *Diwali*. He had hoped to one day bring his family back with him to the United States. Just 49 years old when he died, he was one of six Temple victims of one of the most senseless tragedies in U.S. history, along with his younger brother, Sita Singh.

Shootings in places of worship were certainly not unique, and just seven years earlier in Brookfield, Wisconsin a gunman had killed seven members of his own congregation of the Living Church of God. However, the nature of this shooting, carried out by a white supremacist against one specific group of people, reminded some in the minority communities of the bombings of black churches in the South during the 1960s.

As was the case with most Indians working and traveling back and forth between India and the U.S., obtaining a green card was a necessary requirement to bring their families back to America to stay. Guru and his family had been living in New Delhi, India at the time of the shooting, waiting anxiously for Ranjit's return visit. Guru had looked forward to his father's visit, but after the shocking reality of his death, he came to America to not only see where his father had lived and worked, but to complete his father's story. They had planned to live in America together, and for the members of his family, they would begin the next part of their story after the funeral in Oak Creek.

In the months after the shooting Guru would spend considerable time at the Temple where his father worked, and where he had devoted his life to his faith and to the Temple community. Every Sunday, Guru could be found at the Temple, helping in any way he could, talking with his friends, serving food in the *langar* hall, always stopping at least once to inspect the bullet hole in the door frame of the main Temple hall, the only surviving physical reminder of the shooting.

For Guru staying in America meant enrolling in school, and for him that meant attending Oak Creek High School, just down the street from the Sikh Temple. With a student population of more than 2,000, it is one of the largest high schools in Wisconsin. Many of the children from the Temple went to Oak Creek schools so he had some familiar faces with him in the hallways, someone to speak *Punjabi* with as he began his education.

As a non English-speaking student, Guru struggled to immerse himself in American culture with the additional challenge of being unable to communicate with most of his teachers and fellow students. But his drive to be a part of the world where his father had lived gave him the energy to learn, and he slowly picked up the words and habits of a typical high-schooler, which helped him understand the nuances of life in America. His infectious smile, his willingness to accept what life had handed him and all that he had already experienced, accelerated his learning, giving him at least a chance for a reasonable transition to his new life.

Now, whenever I meet Guru he is an energetic, cheerful, young man. A face I recognized many times as I visited the Temple in the years after the shooting, hearing the stories of his father and the other victims from the families of those killed. His incredible spirit and likability draws people to him, and must have helped him deal with the immense tragedy of losing his father, who he never got to know as a young man, separated by oceans and thousands of miles.

When I had first met Guru, shortly after the funeral services on the Friday after the shootings, he was quick to take a picture of us with his iPhone camera – a selfie with the Mayor he called it – and that had become a tradition every time we would see each other. Initially only able to speak a few words of English — his native language was *Punjabi* — our conversations would eventually center around his experiences and his wide-eyed view of his new life in Oak Creek. Living with his mother and his sister in an apartment just a few blocks from the Temple, it was not unusual to see him riding his bike around the city or when I visited the high school for a sporting event or an assembly.

On the evening of August 5, 2013, in a grass field directly south of the Sikh Temple of Wisconsin, the community came together to commemorate the one-year anniversary of the loss of life at the Temple, and to celebrate the spirit of *Chardi Kala* that had buoyed the spirit of the community since the shooting. Hosted by Amardeep Kaleka, son of the slain Temple president, the event was covered by national and local media and attended by more than 1,000 people. It told the story of the families and the impact of the death of their family members, but also celebrated with music and stories their refusal to fall into despair or to let hate determine the course of the rest of their lives.

Guru, as the son of Ranjit Singh, was called up on the stage to tell his story and to talk about his father. As he began to speak, his emotions welled up and Guru began to sob uncontrollably. At one point Amardeep Kaleka and Kamal Saini stood by his side, telling him to look out into the crowd, who in a show of solidarity with the young Sikh had held up their lighted candles, calming him down, brightening the moment, and getting him through his difficult testimonial to his father.

I had never seen Guru this emotional before, and it was encouraging to see not only his Sikh family embrace him, but also our residents and others from outside Oak Creek. In one overwhelming and uplifting moment on an incredible evening of solidarity and shared experience,

Oak Creek had come together. We had done that on many occasions in the months after the shooting, but this event, celebrated and commemorated with music, storytelling, speeches and tributes to those who had been killed, brought some needed reinforcement to the story of the lost lives, highlighting the amazing recovery by the Sikh community and Oak Creek.

The evening, symbolically framed by an Oak Creek Fire Department ladder truck draped with a very large American flag, the Sikh Temple lit by spotlights behind an open-air stage, gave all of us the chance to come together again. For Guru, it may have been a chance to finally release the emotions he had held so closely inside for his father, who he had never really met.

Meeting each other — Afternoon of August 6, 2012

A few hours after the press conference on Monday, August 6, Chief Edwards and I met with the representatives of the Sikh Temple of Wisconsin in the cafeteria of our local Salvation Army. It was a good choice for the meeting place as there was plenty of room and it offered some degree of privacy from the attention of the media. Since late in the day yesterday, national media had descended on the city and had set up their cameras seemingly everywhere around Oak Creek for their live shots and interviews.

We had conducted the morning's press conference at the police station and the Salvation Army building was only about a half-mile away. Most of us in the room had not formally met each other, and the rawness of Sunday's events still hung in the air, the tension and grief still powerful as we assembled around the tables. We went around the room and introduced ourselves, learning the names and faces we would all come to know very well over the next few months. Temple elders, relatives of the victims, representatives of the federal agencies on scene, Chief Edwards and myself, each of us part of this story.

We had begun by asking the family members from the Temple community what they needed and how we could best help them. Early on, detailed information was still very sketchy and we were questioned on the timing of events and how long it had taken to reach the victims inside the Temple. This was understandable, as many of the victims had been shot multiple times. From the perspective of a grieving family member, any time that it took to provide medical attention could have made the difference between whether their family member lived or died. Chief Edwards explained that emergency medical personnel were allowed in as soon as the scene was deemed to be safe and that all measures that could have been taken were.

At one point a young Sikh man who stood just behind the tables asked about another person of interest, one that had been widely reported about in the first few hours after the shooting. I later learned that this was Kanwardeep Kaleka, the nephew of the slain Temple president Satwant Singh Kaleka. Kanwardeep, or Kanwar, was tall and wore a turban. Unlike most of the other representatives from the Temple in the room, he spoke very good English and was easy to understand. I found out much later that Kanwar was born and raised in the area, just a few miles from the Temple. With an undergraduate degree from the University of Southern California and a PhD student in Milwaukee, he was a youth leader at the Temple and was able to ask the questions that most of the family members wanted answers to. As I listened to him speak, it was clear that he was still very emotional. August 5 for him had been "the longest day of this life," he later told me.

Kanwar recalled that he had barely slept after the shooting, and had spent most of the evening at his uncle's home with his cousins Pardeep and Amardeep Kaleka, the sons of the Temple President. As he lie in bed and fitfully turned over the details of the shooting and the many hours he had spent at Classic Lanes with his family on the evening of August 5, he realized that from that point on, "he had to wear a turban." Since that day, he told me he had taken the *saroop* according to Sikh custom, and pledged to keep his beard untrimmed and his head covered. That night he had even called around, trying to find a turban that he could wear the next day.

In a conversation over a year later, Kanwar told me that over the years he had often struggled with his connection to Sikhism. As a middle school student, one day he suddenly declared to his parents that he was an atheist. Expecting their wrath, he instead received understanding and calm. At USC, his education brought him back to his faith as he connected his spirituality to the wonders of science. His exploration of science had led him to believe "that a universe that is so complex and intricate could not be the product of mere probability, but rather a higher power," Kanwar said.

In that meeting at the Salvation Army, promises were

made between the Chief, the family members, and myself. We talked about honoring the victims so that their lives would not be forgotten, and reassured them that the Temple would be safe in the future and that they would be able to return to their *gurdwara* as soon as possible. To his credit, Chief Edwards and his department worked with the leadership at the Temple and helped to improve the security of the building and grounds. The department consulted with the Temple on many of the safety enhancements made after the shooting.

As I sat there that day and listened to the questions and the calm that was displayed in spite of the extreme brutality that was enacted upon them just hours earlier, it was hard not to want to follow that lead. Vengeance was not part of their reaction and we assured them that we would be there for them as long as they needed us. For many days and months after the shooting, we held meetings with any agency that could provide help; whether it was with law enforcement, counselors, immigration officials, or just a casual conversation over *chai* at the Temple.

The bond that was established that afternoon was built on trust and communication. Any question could be asked and if we didn't have the answer, we worked to find it. Both the Chief and I understood early on that any hesitancy to provide details or information, either to the

Temple community or to the media, could be viewed negatively. We were confident that an open dialogue would be our best course. We reviewed the details, as we knew them, less than 24 hours after Wade Michael Page had entered the Temple, and began the process to move forward.

As the last questions were asked, each of us in the room understood that this was just the beginning of a story that had changed from response to recovery. A quiet prayer for the victims of the shooting ended the meeting.

Kanwar had also begun a change; back to the traditions and customs of his faith. We've talked many times since that afternoon, meeting at the Temple and many other community events. His ability to connect his community with the city leadership that day was an important part of the conversation on August 6. It allowed us to understand each other and to work together to help heal. It demonstrated that we had much more in common than we had differences. I realized that afternoon that much of what we did going forward had significance beyond our city limits. The first step was to bring the communities together and begin the healing process.

National Night Out

The first Tuesday in August celebrates National Night Out, an effort by local police departments to promote crime prevention programs in neighborhoods and to encourage police-community partnerships. In Oak Creek, this has been a very well-attended event over the years, bringing thousands of residents together at the site of the Oak Creek Community Center, located just north of the City Hall complex on Howell Avenue.

With the Temple shooting taking place just two days earlier, we wrestled with the idea of canceling National Night Out, but we decided to hold the event in the effort to keep some normalcy in what had been a very tumultuous 48 hours for our city. At the same time planning for that event continued, we began to talk with the representatives of the Temple about adding an additional memorial piece to the program on Tuesday night, honoring the victims of the shooting. In a two hour meeting with the elders of the Sikh Temple on Monday afternoon, it was very clear that they were interested, but still uncertain as to what this would look like. My initial thoughts were to keep it simple and short, with perhaps an hour of program devoted to the victims and their families. Inside the Temple community, this discussion had taken on even greater significance as the families were preparing not only to mourn their family members who had been killed, but also to honor them in some way.

Each of the victims had a unique and compelling story, and providing that detail about their lives in a manner that was appropriate and compassionate was not an easy task. Monday was very much consumed with the telling of the story of the shooting: who was Wade Michael Page, the six victims, and how was it that they came together on Sunday, August 5?

Police Chief Edwards and I spent the majority of Monday in front of television cameras, and we were still tied up with media requests late into the evening. While we were talking to the press, city staff was beginning to feel the weight of the event in a different way. At City Hall, while some of the employees were gathered in a small break room watching the story unfold on live television, the pressure of an overwhelming level of interest in the story was taxing our phone lines and our ability to respond to these requests for information. Although we had appointed a public information officer, his day was taken up with requests for interviews for the Chief and myself, and everything else was falling on the shoulders of a staff that had not been prepared for an event of this magnitude.

Because all of the victims had ties to India, the level of

interest in that country was unprecedented, and its impact on our small City Hall staff was first felt in the volume of calls we were receiving, and in the number of people accessing our city website and social media sites. Police Chief Edwards had made a comment during the Monday morning press conference that all of the victims' names were published on our home page, which promptly crashed our server and took down our website. Caesar Geiger, Director of Information Technology for the City of Oak Creek, proudly trumpets the fact that they had the site back up and running within a half hour. It was impressive given that India's population is 1.3 billion people, and while the percentage of Sikhs in India is rather small, the Prime Minister at the time of the shooting was a member of the Sikh faith and was acutely aware of our situation here in Oak Creek.

In May of 2012, after my election, I had decided that the city needed to ramp up its digital identity and began the process of creating a city Facebook page and Twitter account. As a candidate I had been active on both, and it surprised me, shocked me really, that our city had not used any new media to improve communication between City Hall and the residents. After several long meetings with staff on the subject of social media and government, it was painfully clear that most people either didn't use it, or were only vaguely familiar with Facebook. The perils of open-records requests, always a challenge for city clerks

due to the record-keeping requirements, slowed the
process, but we finally launched our City of Oak Creek
Facebook page in late May 2012. With the help of our GIS
Coordinator Leslie Flynn, who understood the nuances of
social media, we were ready to use it when needed in
August. The decisions we made in April and May gave us
the flexibility to release information about the shooting
through these additional outlets and relieved some of the
burden on the staff. Victims' names, information about the
city and the Temple, and links to grief counseling and
donations sites were posted to the social media sites
within 24 hours, providing an important resource to the
public, curious not only about where Oak Creek was, but
what they could do to help.

Throughout the day Monday, staff had begun to formulate
a plan for a vigil to be held just after the National Night
Out event, in Miller Park, a small city-owned park named
after the family who had donated the land to the city. It
was directly adjacent to the Oak Creek Community Center
and a short walk from the City Hall building. Miller Park
was just a few acres in size, but its location provided a
logical choice to host the vigil, and as Monday's
conversations developed, it was obvious that this would
be much larger event than the Chief and I had proposed.
Our decision to let the Temple community drive the
planning and logistics for the vigil proved to be a smart
one. They were tuned into the significance of this event in

their own community, which was still reeling from Sunday's shooting, our residents, who shared fears and concerns, and a national and international audience, who would see and hear about the event in the overwhelming media coverage that night.

Two younger members from the Temple took leadership roles in the planning, and each provided cultural and faith-based insight into the Sikh community that we would have been unable to gather on our own. Gurmukh Mangat and Gurpreet Kaur Dulai spent much of Monday and Tuesday in or around City Hall, providing key details on what the vigil should look like, and also arranging the staging, lighting, sound and other details that ultimately would make this event historic, not only for our city, but in the scope of its impact on the greater Sikh community. They recruited many of their peers from the Temple, and I remember walking through the council chambers on Tuesday, watching them cut head scarves for the vigil from hundreds of yards of fabric hastily purchased from JoAnn Fabrics. Each member of the public would be encouraged to cover their heads as they attended the vigil on Tuesday night, a display of solidarity with the Temple community, honoring the traditions of their faith.

On Monday evening, Chief Edwards and I had a brief meeting at City Hall with City Clerk Catherine Roeske, City Administrator Jerry Peterson, as well as a few other members of City Hall staff to review where the plans stood for the vigil Tuesday night. I remember pushing back a bit when I heard that the vigil might run as long as two and a half hours, but ultimately, the event was going to be what it was, and the timing and the length would be influenced by the crowd and what the organizers from the Temple wanted to present at the event. Security was an issue for the vigil as well, as there was still uncertainty about the motives of Wade Michael Page, and who else might be out there, newly encouraged to take action against members of the Sikh community. The police department had been running on empty since the shooting, and now we were asking them to provide security to thousands of people, in a public park, at night. No easy task with our staffing options low, given how many officers had been involved in the police response on Sunday and were now off-duty, several of them dealing with their own stress.

One of the little known back-stories about the night of the vigil was that Officer Sam Lenda, who had stopped Wade Michael Page's rampage on Sunday morning, was moving through the crowd Tuesday night, and at one point I looked over and saw him in the park, nodded in his direction, not wanting to call attention to his presence there. The fact that Lenda wanted to be part of the vigil, given all that had transpired on Sunday, is a shining example of what makes him the officer he is, the perfect person to meet the challenge on Sunday, and to represent the department. Not many police departments across the country would expect their most senior officer to be at center stage in a mass-casualty incident, but Sam Lenda was the easy choice. An expert marksman and emergency response instructor, his actions on Sunday, August 5 provided a checklist for proper police procedure, and demonstrated his unwavering commitment to the principles of his profession.

Tuesday, August 7 was a somber day in Oak Creek, but the sun was still shining brightly in the late afternoon, the temperature almost perfect for August. If we were going to have thousands of people show up and stand outside at the vigil for the Sikh Temple victims, it was encouraging to know that the weather wouldn't be an obstacle. Residents began showing up at the grounds of the Oak Creek Community Center shortly before 5:00 p.m., and at this stage of the evening, it was moving forward as a typical National Night Out; police dog demonstrations, safety presentations, and families with children moving through the exhibits spread out across the parking lot of the Community Center.

Late in the afternoon on Tuesday, sitting in my office, I had begun the process of working out some comments for the event that night. I would be one of several speakers at the vigil, with Wisconsin Governor Scott Walker, Police Chief Edwards, Nirupama Rao, the Indian Ambassador to the

United States, along with a member of each victim's family, who would read a bio of their family member.

My wife Kathy, who had been working behind the scenes at home to make sure all of my immediate family members were up to speed on the latest information and my well-being, sat in my office, helping me as I struggled to find the right words. I knew what I wanted to say, but hitting the right points was important and I wanted to be clear about our future course. This was an event that shocked our city, and I wanted the world to know that we would not become a statistic, or just another city that had suffered a tragedy. I thought it was important to talk about the diversity of Oak Creek, at a time when a group of people who looked differently from the rest of us had been violated in the worst possible way, at their place of worship, doing nothing more than celebrating their faith on a quiet, Sunday morning.

We went back and forth as Kathy typed the words, changing a word here, adding a phrase there, refining what would be a relatively short speech, but one that would carry great significance to our residents, and to the large number of Sikh Americans who would also be attending the vigil from many places outside of Oak Creek. Throughout the day, we had received calls from many Sikh organizations asking about the details of the vigil, and we were already aware of several busloads of people coming in from Indiana and Illinois. City staff had already developed a parking and shuttle plan in advance of their arrival to ensure that they could get to the vigil safely and without hassle. City Administrator Jerry Peterson had to make on-the-spot decisions on allocating resources to ensure that the vigil went off without a hitch, and each of those decisions went a long way in the ultimate success of the event on Tuesday night. Staff was directly involved in arranging the staging, lighting and sound system for the Miller Park site, as well as working with Walgreens and other companies who donated the candles for the participants to hold during the vigil.

Miller Park is a small, community park located just east of the Community Center, and a block north of City Hall. Filled with tall elm and oak trees and a darkly-stained park pavilion building situated on a pond annually stocked with trout, it was a perfect location for the vigil. Its location was important for many reasons, but principally it was immediately adjacent to the Community Center, which was playing host to National Night Out. In years past, residents would participate in a flashlight walk from the Community Center parking lot, east to Oak Creek High School's stadium, for a fireworks presentation. This year, because of the tragic events of Sunday, the fireworks were being replaced by the vigil, and candles would illuminate the short walk for the thousands of people who were there. The vigil would be the first opportunity many of our residents would have to publicly grieve with each other and demonstrate a show of support for the victim's families and for our wounded officer Lt. Brian Murphy.

As I walked through the parking lot at the Community Center in the early evening on Tuesday, I was warmly greeted by the residents, many asking how I was doing or thanking me for the comments I made during the press conferences on Sunday and Monday. I had only been the Mayor for less than four months, but the incident thrust me into a role not typical of the position, at least not before August 5. Just like the Temple family members had done, this show of compassion was something that stuck out in my mind, and gave me a sense that we were hitting the right notes in our response to the tragic events on Sunday.

One of the things that most people notice when an event like this takes place is that elected officials usually show up, some using the opportunity as a means to further their own particular goals or ideology. On Tuesday night, August 7, United States Congressman Paul Ryan of Wisconsin, whose Congressional district Oak Creek falls in, was one of the first on the scene, not to use the event as a platform, but just to talk with residents and to reassure our community. We met briefly on the Community Center grounds and he offered his help and that of his office. When I asked him if he wanted to speak at the vigil, he politely declined, telling me that he was really just there to support our community. What we weren't aware of that night, although the decision had already been made, was that less than a week later, on August 12, he would be selected by Presidential candidate Mitt Romney as his choice for vice president on the 2012 Republican ticket.

As National Night Out wound down, the national anthem was played by a Salvation Army band on a small stage in the parking lot, just under the U.S. and State of Wisconsin flags flying at half mast, under Presidential order, for the victims of the shooting. A photo of that scene eventually would become the banner picture for our website and social media sites for the next six months. It honored the victims, but symbolized the strength of our community and our willingness to embrace the larger questions of how we respond to tragedies, and what role we can play in reducing the likelihood of incidents like this happening in the future.

One by one, other national and local political leaders arrived, U.S. Senator Herb Kohl, Wisconsin Governor Scott Walker, Milwaukee Mayor Tom Barrett, Milwaukee County Executive Chris Abele, and many Wisconsin State Senators and Assembly Representatives. Each had expressed their condolences and shared sense of grief over the events of Sunday, and also extended the power and resources of their offices. I was impressed by their willingness to be there for our community, and to stand with me in front of our residents on a stage, sharing our grief, while collectively mourning the victims of Sunday's shooting. As the sun set in a striking visual display of orange and light blue hues, the large crowd slowly moved across the street to the park, stopping at several candle and head scarf stations, run by city staff, members of the Sikh community, and local volunteers. The park, lit by spotlights powered by humming generators illuminating the canopy of tall trees, took on an almost mystical appearance, highlighted by the colorful dress of the members of the Sikh faith, who were showing up in large numbers. One of my clearest memories of this night is looking out across a field of faces, saddened by the events of Sunday, August 5, each wearing a head covering, holding a lit candle, searching for some answers to why this happened, and how they would cope with it.

Gurmukh Mangat, who had literally worked around the clock planning every detail of this community gathering since Monday afternoon, was now in full command of the Tuesday night vigil, and most of the logistical planning and the order of events were handled by him. Enthusiastic, forceful and insistent on the specifics of what needed to happen on Tuesday night, he began to take charge of the site, at one point corralling every political figure on the scene into the Miller Park pavilion, herding all of us onto picnic benches, a scene as politically unlikely as I'd ever seen. Democrats and Republicans, often-bitter political opponents, were now sitting quietly together, walked through the evening's schedule by a young Sikh man who at one point extolled everyone to "quiet down and listen." It was a testament to the passion he felt for what he was doing, and for what his local Sikh Temple family had gone through since Sunday morning.

Governor Walker and Mayor Tom Barrett of Milwaukee, who had run against each other in the election for Governor of Wisconsin in 2010, were seated next to each other, both wearing a headscarf to show their solidarity with the Sikhs.

If there were a picture of the scene that night, one that would capture everyone's attention immediately, it would be that every person in that building was wearing a head covering. For many of us, it was the first time we had ever done that. It was important that the event honored the traditions of the Sikh faith, and for them, that gesture showed respect and equality. Initially, some of the elected officials showed some hesitation in putting one on, expressing concerns about not wanting to offend other faith groups, an awkward, but misguided attempt at political correctness, I guess. I'll always believe that most people, when put in the position to make a choice to help solve a problem, or in this case, ease the suffering of a large group of people, will do the right thing, and that was clearly the case on that night.

As I left the Oak Creek Community Center, and walked over to the vigil site, crossing Knights Place, the street named after the local high school's mascot, and into the park, the enormity and the magnitude of the event began to sink in. Thousands of residents, people from the surrounding communities, and busses full of Sikhs from around the country were pouring into the park, creating some immediate traffic and parking issues, but all there to show their solidarity and support to the victims and their families.

The area around the stage, set up facing east across an open spot in the park, had already filled up, a sea of brightly colored turbans, head scarves and women's saris and *salwar kameez*, the traditional clothing from the Punjab area of India. On the stage, the Overpass Light Brigade, a volunteer group most famously known for protesting against sitting Wisconsin Governor Scott Walker during the contentious debate over Wisconsin's Budget Repair Bill, or Act 10, were displaying lighted sign panels with the words "Practice Peace." They were on the same stage where Governor Walker would speak less than an hour later. Even with the bitter partisanship of the past year in Wisconsin, on that night everyone in attendance was focused on the same thing and stood on the same side. Speakers, guests, and family members began to climb the short steps onto the stage, the music of Sikh prayers playing in the background, and each of us took a place directly behind the podium.

Two of the major national Sikh organizations, the Sikh Coalition and the Sikh American Legal Defense and Education Fund, were represented in Oak Creek by Amardeep Singh, co-founder of the Sikh Coalition, and Jasjit Singh, Executive Director of SALDEF, two men who had been on the ground within 24 hours of the shooting at the Temple. They provided valuable insight into the Sikh community to both Chief Edwards and myself, helped us understand the tenets and customs of their faith, and pointed us in the right direction on where to dedicate our resources and support. Both men understood the significance of Sunday's events from the Sikh perspective, but they also had a profound knowledge of what the event could mean in future conversations about equality, religious freedom, and respect in our country. Much like the bombings of black churches in the 1960s, this act of hate and violence was enacted at a place of worship toward a group of people who looked differently and in this case prayed differently. It would also trigger calls for civil rights hearings in Washington, D.C., ultimately leading to the inclusion of Sikh Americans in the FBI's categorization of hate crime statistics.

Amardeep Singh was selected by the Temple elders to lead

the vigil, and as he began to speak, I could feel the overwhelming grief and sadness of the moment begin to overcome me, momentarily shifting my thoughts away from what I was preparing to talk about when I addressed the crowd. I lost my legs a bit, and leaned on a member of the Temple standing to my left. After two days of very little sleep, high emotion, and an incredible sense of loss and grief, I was beginning to show signs of wear. My wife had noticed this earlier when she listened to my voice on a radio interview, noting that I sounded very tired. Sleep had eluded me, and I was running on adrenalin and coffee, and not much else.

I later learned that the man standing to my left was Balhair Dulai, one of the Temple elders and a 30-year resident of Oak Creek. He was a business owner and an important voice representing the Temple that night. Dulai has a long, dark black beard, untrimmed in the custom of Sikhs, and looks very serious, even when he's not. As I wavered, he put his arm around me, steadying me, calming me. That moment is something that I've carried with me from that day forward – an example of a simple act of kindness, done with compassion and without hesitation, for a complete stranger. I've thought about that simple gesture many times since, and it continues to impress upon me the importance of reaching out beyond your own family and friends, to help out someone who is outside your own circle of life, and who may need a helping hand.

As I was introduced to the crowd, I pulled my notes out of my back pocket and quickly realized that despite the large print on the page and without my glasses, I would not be able to read this speech. I typically don't like to wear my glasses when I'm speaking in front of a crowd, probably more out of a sense of vanity than anything else. This time I would need to remember what I had composed just an hour earlier. Simultaneously introducing the other dignitaries on stage as I mentally reconstructed my words, I was able to speak to the importance of what this night meant for not only the family members of the victims, but also to our residents, many of whom had never met a person from the Sikh faith before. Going back to what Mayor Hogan had told me two days earlier; I went with what I knew.

Text of my speech at the Sikh Temple Vigil, Miller Park, Oak Creek, Wisconsin August 7, 2012:

> *Traditionally, National Night Out has been an event promoting public safety, community pride, and stronger police and community relationships. The events of Sunday, August 5, have demonstrated how important those values are in a community like Oak Creek and across our country.*
>
> *Tonight we mourn the victims of the Sikh Temple shooting and grieve with their families. We pray for*

*the safety of our wounded officer Lt. Brian Murphy
and we honor the heroic efforts of our police, fire,
and other first responders.*

*As a community, we will not let this single tragic
event define who we are. It will only serve to build a
stronger resolve against senseless violence and
hatred. Our healing process begins tonight when
we come together, joining hands to celebrate the
diversity of our city, which enriches our lives. Join
me in embracing that diversity.*

I spoke that night and was confident in the words, but not
in my delivery of them. I had never given a speech with the
importance of that one, and as I look back on that time, I
realize how the events have changed me. Despite my
career choice, as the mayor of a city of 35,000 people, the
gravity and significance of a mass shooting is not one you
can train for, and even if you could, I'm not sure it would
make any difference. If I've gotten any better on delivering
these types of speeches since, it's due to familiarity with
the subject and my passion for it. The messages of
diversity, mutual respect, and acceptance are important,
and I began to talk about them in earnest at the vigil that
night. I'm committed to making that part of the story the
long lasting legacy of the shooting.

Governor Walker was next on stage, and his comments

echoed what others would say that night – we had come together that night to join as a community, all kinds of people representing different faiths but sharing a feeling that despite our differences, we showed that we could support and look out for each other. During his remarks, the Governor noted that he had just been notified that his wife Tonette had been rushed into surgery, and that he would be leaving right after his stop in Oak Creek. His appearance played a role in reducing the fears of our residents and helped to calm the situation, which two days later was still very raw. It was important that the leader of our state was there that night, despite all the political hostilities of the last year, and I've thanked him for that visit every time I've seen him since.

Standing on the small stage, filled with politicians, members of the victims' families, representatives of Sikh organizations and law enforcement agencies, it was remarkable to see the faces of all the people in the crowd, each quietly holding their candles. As the speakers came forward, they listened attentively, giving the Sikh version of a shout-out, loudly proclaiming, "*Bole So Nihal, Sati Sri Akal,*" after Chief Edwards and others spoke, indicating collective respect and praise for their words and actions. The Indian Ambassador, a woman who had traveled all the way from India to attend the vigil and the services on Friday, mentioned that four of the victims were Indian citizens; some had just recently arrived in the country. One of the family members, Gurvinder Singh, had barely known his father and had been looking forward to a visit with him just a few months later, a visit that now would never take place.

Gurpreet Kaur Dulai, a twenty-something pharmacy student, representing the youth group from the Temple, spoke about the fund-raising efforts of the community to help the families, some of whom had very little resources. Her voice was shaky, still hurting from Sunday's events, but brave enough to step on stage in front of thousands of people. Later I learned her father was Balhair Dulai, who stood next to me on stage and helped me through that night.

Jasjit Singh read the biographies of each of the victims slowly, with detail of their births and histories, both in India and in America, and how they were part of the fabric of the Temple and of their greater Sikh community. He explained the traditions and tenets of the Sikh faith, the spirit of *Chardi Kala*, which means relentless optimism and joy, and how it related to the kindness and compassion of a people who despite having suffered so greatly were able to react with peace. They chose not to act out in anger at the extreme hatred and violence directed towards them two days earlier. Chief Edwards and I had both noted during our time with the members of the Temple that each of them was concerned with our well being, at one point asking us if we were OK. I had been impressed with their calmness in the face of such adversity, and they truly demonstrated their faith, even at the toughest moments of their lives. Citing Sikh scripture, he said the words, "fear none, frighten none," and repeated them with emphasis, telling the crowd that the Sikhs were part of this "country of immigrants" and that this event would not deter them or shake their spirit or faith.

The last speaker of the night was Amardeep Kaleka, son of Satwant Singh Kaleka, slain President of the Sikh Temple of Wisconsin, a Temple his father had helped build in 2007. It gave the Sikh community a permanent home in Oak Creek after years of rented spaces in public parks and other buildings scattered around the Milwaukee area. Amardeep, a film maker living in Southern California, had emerged as the public spokesman for the families, making appearances with CNN's Anderson Cooper and MSNBC's Rachel Maddow on Monday evening, providing depth and background into the Sikh American experience for many Americans who had little or no knowledge of the Sikh faith, or what they represented to the American story. Amardeep spoke about the shared experience of losing a loved one, and his words were a perfect closure to the evening, calming the crowd, and easing the deep pain of the loss of these six members of our community, who before Sunday, were unknown to most of us.

As the vigil came to an end, the crowd slowly filtered out, disappearing past the edges of the lit park and into the night, the bright colors slowly fading to grey. It had brought us together to begin to heal from Sunday's shooting, but the impact was far greater than that. Each of us there that night were beginning to see the real legacy of the shootings, one that Wade Michael Page never intended. We were coming together as a community with a shared experience beyond violence, connecting our personal histories, cultures, and faiths.

Lt. Brian Murphy — Six Minutes

Lt. Brian Murphy probably had no idea his life would be changed forever on August 5, 2012, but as every public safety officer is well aware, every shift brings with it an element of danger and the unknown. When he volunteered to fill-in for a co-worker that Sunday, he probably assumed his day would be filled with the typical calls he'd seen throughout this career in Oak Creek. His shift on that day started at 7:00 a.m. and right up until 10:26 a.m. that morning his day consisted of routine calls and general paperwork.

Murphy, a 21 year veteran of the Oak Creek Police Department, responded that morning to an initial dispatcher call of a possible fight, quickly escalating to shots fired, which prompted him to respond with lights and sirens running to the Temple on south Howell Avenue. As he drove up the driveway, he noticed two individuals essentially lying on top of each other adjacent to a vehicle and next to the low retaining wall, which runs along the north side of the parking lot. He checked them quickly and noticed there were no apparent signs of life.

As he looked up, he noticed an individual wearing a t-shirt, eventually identified as the shooter Wade Michael Page, jogging from the front door of the Temple, and moving directly toward him into the parking lot. Without warning,

Page immediately fired on Murphy, striking him in the jaw. Murphy fired back once, and scrambled for cover behind an adjacent car, never losing his awareness of Page or where he was in relation to him. When Page came around the car, Murphy stood up, and Page began shooting again. He was hit by another shot, this time the bullet taking off part of the tip of his left thumb, and knocking the gun out of his hand. In classic Murphy fashion, he thought to himself, "Damn, this is going to leave a mark," his humor never leaving him even in this moment of incredible danger.

When I talked with him months later, he believed he put into practice the self-preservation training he had learned in his many years of law enforcement training, tucking his head under the vehicle as much possible, preventing Page from killing him. While he was in this position, Page stood over him, continually fired into his body, eventually shooting him at least 17 times, including three directly into his armored vest, which undoubtedly saved his life.

Murphy, the son of a garbage man and a bank manager who grew up in Brooklyn, comes from a family steeped in law enforcement. His grandfather was a captain with the New York Police Department, his brother Terence, a retired detective, and his sister-in-law is also a police officer. One of four children – he had two older sisters and a younger brother – Murphy was 24 years old when his mother died. Murphy grew up in some tough Brooklyn neighborhoods, and his upbringing served him well as he joined the Marines after high school. He served tours in Afghanistan and New Delhi, India, and these experiences provided him some early insight into the Indian culture that he called upon after the shooting, as he met many citizens of India and transplants to the U.S. who sought him out to personally thank him after the shooting. After his military career, he served as a Jefferson County Deputy Sheriff in Southeast Wisconsin before accepting a position with the Oak Creek Police Department.

On his release date from Froedtert Hospital on August 22, 2012, just 17 days after he was critically wounded in the Temple shooting, I watched Murphy as he walked out of the hospital under his own power through an undisclosed back door of the hospital, purposely kept under wraps to avoid the media. Surrounded by family members and many of his co-workers at the Oak Creek police department, Murphy greeted each person and thanked them individually for being there. It was a tremendous scene that afternoon, with tears shed and shouts of support coming from the two lines of people, the emotions of the moment welling up as he walked through the crowd, eventually getting into his family's van with his wife Ann.

As I talked with Murphy in the months after his release

from the hospital, his recovery still a work in progress, he spoke about his childhood and lessons he learned growing up in a diverse community. He mentioned a local coach in his Pop Warner football league who gave him some solid life lessons and encouragement. He talked about a training accident in 2009 that almost cost him his law-enforcement career, and how he somehow talked his way back into active-duty, setting the stage for the events of August 5, 2012. He considers himself a more spiritual person now, both from his experiences at the Sikh Temple of Wisconsin and the fact that he still carries relics from that day, a bullet lodged in his skull and another in his neck serving as permanent reminders of how close he came to death.

On Tuesday evening, February 12, 2013, Murphy was honored as a special guest of President Barack Obama at his State of the Union address. I watched the broadcast on television that night as Murphy, seated next to First Lady Michele Obama, was recognized by the President near the end of his speech. Here is an excerpt from the President's comments that night.

> *"We should follow the example of a police officer named Brian Murphy. When a gunman opened fire on a Sikh temple in Wisconsin and Brian was the first to arrive, he did not consider his own safety. He fought back until help arrived and ordered his fellow officers to protect the safety of*

the Americans worshiping inside, even as he lay bleeding from 12 bullet wounds. And when asked how he did that, Brian said, "That's just the way we're made."

Murphy's heroism has been honored many times since August 5, 2012. He and fellow officer Sam Lenda have received nearly every national award in law enforcement, and many others from the Sikh community, who consider them both heroes. Through all of this attention and focus on his unselfish and brave actions on the day of the shooting, he remains committed to restoring some normalcy to his life, interrupted only by that six-minute exchange with Wade Michael Page. After months of operations and many walks around the block with his wife Ann and their dog in their Bay View, Wisconsin neighborhood, he's slowly getting back to normal. For Murphy, that's the best part of all.

Sikh Services — Friday August 10th

A small sign hanging just above the entrance inside the large gymnasium at Oak Creek High School reads *Capacity 2340*, and on Friday, August 10, it was filled to capacity throughout the morning with thousands of people who attended the funeral services of the six slain members of the Sikh Temple of Wisconsin. As the largest venue in the city, and just across Knights Place, a short walk from Oak Creek City Hall, it was the only building large enough to handle the volume of people converging on the city for the services. In the first few days after the shooting, it was agreed upon by the School District that it would be the site for the public visitation and memorial service for the victims. This was important to the Temple families, but also to our residents, who were still grieving, just five days after Wade Michael Page had carried out his murderous rampage.

Inside the gym, six wooden caskets were placed side by side under one of the basketball hoops, family members positioned at the sides of each of them. Most were still in shock, others cried, some interacted with the mourners paying their respects as they slowly walked past, the music of Sikh prayers playing in the background. Above their heads was a large screen displaying the pictures of the victims and our wounded police officer, Lt. Brian Murphy, still lying in Froedtert Hospital, recovering from his wounds.

Outside the high school, the line of people waiting to get inside stretched around the corner and across the parking lot. Many of the mourners wore headscarves in respect to the Sikh community. In the line were people from all around the country, some from as far away as California, and many from England and India, home to many members of the Sikh faith, who had traveled to Oak Creek to show their respect to the families.

Dr. Sara Burmeister, Superintendent of the Oak Creek School District, had facilitated the use of the school buildings for the memorial service. In discussions with the victims' families throughout the week she had worked out many of the details, including the logistics of moving thousands of people through the gym, while balancing the safety of the mourners, the families, and hundreds of media members covering the event. Choosing the school site for the services was not an easy decision given that schools typically are safe havens not associated with acts of violence. For the Temple community, the location made sense. It was located nearby, could accommodate the large crowds coming for the six funerals, and was well known by the Sikh community, many of their children having attended school there.

The Superintendent had been concerned about establishing a precedent, since they had never allowed a funeral on school district property before, although requests had been made previously for students who had died. Given the nature of this event and the circumstances surrounding it, she ultimately decided that it was in the best interests of the community and the families of the victims to make the high school gym available for the services. Two weeks later, she would open up the school again, this time for a historic visit from First Lady Michelle Obama.

As arrangements evolved during the week, and as dignitary and media requests came in, juggling the expectations of everyone involved was challenging. Significant security concerns highlighted that list. The Justice Department, FBI, and the Governor's office each had specific needs, and like a lot of activity associated with a mass shooting, it was unfamiliar territory for all of us.

In an email almost a year later, the Superintendent shared some of her recollections from that day: "During the services, one of the challenges was determining who was family, and who wasn't. It said a great deal about their community — they consider everyone family — but for someone whose job it was to prevent people from going past the barricade where the families were, it was hard to do. We tried to do this as gently and respectfully as possible, understanding what people were feeling," Burmeister recalled.

Reporters from international news organizations, national media, and nearly every local television and radio station had filled up the roped-off area designated for the media on the opposite side of the gym. Despite the restrictions, many of the reporters were savvy enough to pass themselves off as mourners, including one reporter from the local NBC affiliate who took a picture of me as I sat in the bleachers wearing a head scarf, a picture which later showed up on the local news broadcast. At this point, my picture had been taken hundreds of times in the past week and I was getting used to it, but in this setting, it seemed inappropriate. Overall, the treatment of Oak Creek by the media, both local and national, had been positive, perhaps a signal that our commitment to honor nearly any and all requests for information had paid off.

Chief Edwards and I arrived together at the services that morning and slowly made our way to the front of the gym, the bleachers and folding chairs set up on the basketball court already full with mourners. I had spent many hours with the family members since Sunday, and recognized many of them now as I slowly walked past each coffin, offering my condolences, and stopping to embrace them. Each greeting was somber and emotionally overwhelming, especially when I came up to Kamal and

Saini, whose mother Paramjit Kaur was the only woman killed in the attack. She had been praying in the *gurdwara* when Wade Michael Page had arrived on Sunday and was getting up from prayer when she was shot in the back. She died in the prayer hall of the *gurdwara*. Their family had just returned from a visit to India a month before the shooting, their first together since immigrating to the United States eight years earlier. Both young men showed tremendous grief in their faces. Heavy with the loss of someone so close and so loved, their courage at this time helped in their healing, and ultimately would put them front and center at a Washington, D.C. Senate Committee hearing on civil rights just two months later.

If the community vigil on Tuesday night had started the grieving process for the residents, the memorial service on Friday was an opportunity for each member of the community to pass their condolences to the family members directly, a remarkable display of shared grief, given that most residents had never interacted with members of the Sikh Temple before this week. Each day after the shooting, the outpouring of support from people inside and outside the city had been remarkable. Flowers and gift boxes had been arriving at the police department non-stop since Monday, and had begun to fill the office of Chief Edwards and at City Hall. Thousands of emails, letters, and phone calls filled our in-boxes, each with a similar message of condolence, some of which we made available for the public to see in a large display case adjacent to the City Clerk's counter at City Hall.

While the memorial service was a solemn event, it was also very public. Attorney General Eric Holder, Wisconsin Governor Scott Walker, and Jesse Jackson each spoke at a short ceremony during the service. In his comments, the Attorney General called the shooting an "act of terrorism" and a "hate crime," words the Sikh community had been waiting to hear, having suffered considerably in the years after 9/11, and in some cases, losing their lives in the process. Balbir Singh Sodhi had been murdered four days after 9/11, while planting flowers at his gas station in Mesa, Arizona. In the Sikh community, this was perceived as an act of retaliation after the 9/11 attacks, a claim backed up by the U.S. Justice Department. It was the first of dozens of hate crime murders and other incidents towards Sikhs in the years since 9/11.

Attorney General Holder didn't use the opportunity to make a link between the mass shooting and gun control, a subject that had begun to gain momentum in the media since Sunday, and a discussion which would eventually take me all the way to the White House in January of 2013. He was appearing on behalf of the President, and his visit may have been scheduled to assuage the Sikh Community. I had heard concerns that some members of the Sikh community were upset that the President had not come to

Oak Creek, especially in light of his visit to Aurora a week prior. Many Temple members viewed the attack on their Temple as just as significant as the bombings of black churches in the 1960s civil rights era. Given that it was one of the worst mass shootings in our country's history, and had taken place inside a place of worship, it was hard to disagree with them.

Wisconsin Governor Scott Walker, who had also attended the vigil in Oak Creek on Tuesday night, spoke about the reaction of the Temple families after the shootings and their calmness in the face of overwhelming grief and sadness. "This week, our friends in the Sikh community have shown us the best way to respond is with love," he said, echoing what most of us had already recognized in our meetings with the Sikh community throughout the week. I had seen it firsthand, and I wasn't sure I could have held back my anger as well as they had, given how their lives had been torn apart. In conversations with representatives of the Sikh community at the national level in the first week after the shooting, I had heard again and again the spirit of *Chardi Kala* invoked. If there is a perception that Oak Creek had done something right in its response to the shooting, the spirit of cooperation and compassion demonstrated by the Sikh community were one of the principal reasons for that.

While Attorney General Holder and Governor Walker had

focused their comments on the Sikh community, Jesse Jackson, a civil rights leader whose appearances often trigger as much public comment as his own words, didn't shy away from linking the shooting to a call for gun control. At one point, he called for restrictions on gun access to prevent future massacres, remarks he made just before delivering the closing prayer for the funeral service. His presence in a very conservative pro-gun city like Oak Creek probably raised some eyebrows in the community and I'm not sure that he should have raised the issue in the immediate days after the shooting. For me, the first week was about healing and recovery, and stirring the pot on gun control certainly could have had the opposite effect. His comments were probably intended for a national audience and eventually found their way into the national news coverage of the shooting and a larger political discussion. I had the opportunity to meet with Jackson on Thursday, at a public forum sponsored by the Department of Justice, and he did personally express his condolences and support for our community.

As each victim's family members came forward and talked about their loved ones, Pardeep Kaleka, a former City of Milwaukee policeman and the eldest son of the slain Temple President, Satwant Kaleka, urged the community to "not fight hate with hate." He would use that concept again months later when he helped found *Serve2Unite*. The grassroots organization brings together a diverse group of interfaith youth to help at-risk communities spread cross-cultural awareness, volunteering at many community events across the area, their colorful t-shirts with a bloody hand print splashed across the front announcing their presence.

As he talked about his father, and as the other family members related their own memories to the audience seated in the folding chairs and bleachers of the gym, the emotional weight of the scene was significant. Many in the crowd wiped away tears and consoled others seated next to them. At one point during the service, several of the police officers who were the first to respond on Sunday walked through the receiving line to pay their respect to the families, many of whom embraced them, thanking them for their service. This bond between the Police Department and the members of the Sikh Temple of Wisconsin was strong, strengthened by the story of Murphy, who had risked his own life in order to save the lives of the men, women and children still inside the Temple when he arrived on the scene Sunday, August 5, shortly after 10:28 a.m.

In the days and months after the shooting, this bond would grow. At Chief Edwards' direction, the officers would often stop in the parking lot of the Temple as they wrote their shift reports, sometimes stopping inside to have a cup of *chai*, checking in on the members as their lives slowly returned to routine. Just like the Police Department, the Temple is always staffed, a member on hand to greet a visitor, explaining Sikhism and the workings of the Temple, or provide a free *langar* meal for someone who was hungry. This relationship provided a template for a future understanding of the role of law enforcement in the safety and security of faith groups and other institutions in our community.

As Chief Edwards and I left the service, the line of mourners still extending out the door, Doug Seymour, our acting public information officer after the shooting, rushed us off to another series of interviews. This week had seen unprecedented attention on our city, with a sharp focus on a group who had done nothing to deserve the attention, but under that microscope had shown all of us the healing power of kindness, and a willingness to rise above personal tragedy. One tenet of the Sikh faith is service to the community. That week they had opened up our eyes to the importance of that value, not only for their members, but also to the rest of us. In the coming months, they would welcome me into the Temple, a place before August 5, 2012, I had only driven past.

Meeting the Sikhs

Visitors to the Sikh Temple of Wisconsin have to drive up a long, gradual hill to reach the Temple, the elevation concealing the 17,000 square foot, cream-colored brick building from the road. Until August 5, 2012, this fact gave the members a measure of anonymity in the community. A remodeled farmhouse sits to the right of the driveway to the property, further hiding the Temple from the thousands of drivers who pass by each day on Howell Avenue, to and from their homes and jobs. It's the same driveway that the members of the Temple use each week to come to worship, the path that Wade Michael Page took to carry out his murderous rampage, the same route Murphy and Officer Sam Lenda drove up on their way to ending it.

When I first came up the drive, a few weeks after the shooting, it was hard not to carry the images I had seen from the squad car dash-cam videos with me. Those images told the story of what happened on the outside of the building on the morning of August 5. Murphy's dash-cam showed the two victims lying at the bottom of a low retaining wall on the northern edge of the parking lot, his immediate confrontation with Page which caused him to dive for cover to his right, behind the vehicle where Page would eventually fire more than a dozen shots into his body. Lenda's dash-cam showed Page approaching his arrival on the drive with extreme agitation, causing Lenda to reverse back down the drive, and quickly taking a defensive position. When he advanced again and got out of his squad car, Page shot and struck the squad windshield, spraying broken glass over Lenda.

These images, along with the never-released dash-cam video of Murphy being hauled into the back of another squad car, were hard to shake. As I arrived in the parking lot, my eyes moved to each of these locations, eventually parking only a few spots away from where Lenda had taken Page down with a shot to his body. Shortly after, Page had taken his own life. Having spent the last three weeks living with the aftermath of the shooting, and revisiting the event each day through interview requests and news stories, it was both emotional and encouraging to see life slowly returning to normal at the Temple. The lot, nearly full with the vehicles of Temple members attending Sunday services, had resumed its normal role, the remnants of the violence of the events of August 5 now washed away with rain and the passage of time.

The entrance to the Temple features an arched drive-up directly in front of the main doors, leading to a brightly lit entry hall. On my arrival that morning in late August 2012, small children from the Temple were running back and forth and wove through the other members of the Temple, who periodically stepped out from the services. Sikh services typically run for more than two hours on most weekends. Two of the expectations for visitors to the Temple are that you remove your shoes and cover your head, both acts of respect. I had already been aware of the requirement to cover your head, having done that at both the vigil and the services right after the shooting.

Dr. Navdeep Singh Gill, one of the elders of the Temple, a burly but gentle man in his mid-fifties, greeted me warmly as I walked through the main doors. He immediately directed me to the area directly adjacent to the entryway on the left, where members and visitors could remove and place their shoes on the long racks along the wall. Many male members of the Temple wear turbans, the traditional head covering that male Sikhs have worn for centuries. The Temple always provides bandannas in a box just inside the door, so that visitors can quickly cover their heads before stepping into the Temple's main prayer hall.

I had alerted the Temple elders of my visit with my wife Kathy and a few members of City Hall staff. We were warmly embraced by many members of the Temple community, who were gathered in an informal receiving line in the entryway. We had gone through a lot together in the past few weeks, and it was nice to finally be able to stop at the Temple and spend some time with the members informally, outside the glare of the media. Many of the Temple community members who I had met over the last few weeks were there that day. The mood was elevated after the grief and sadness of the shooting. They were putting their lives back together, sorting out details of immigration status of family members, and returning their day-to-day activities to normal.

When you enter the Temple you are immediately struck by the rainbow of color, the head coverings and clothing of the Sikhs truly one of the most beautiful aspects of their Temple life. The palette of colors created an almost impressionistic scene full of youth, families, and faith. The image softened the impact of what happened here just a few weeks earlier. It struck me then, as it does every time I visit the Temple, that different faiths hold so many similarities. The tenets may be different, their histories radically so, but scenes of faith have much in common. Most people who dare to take the time to step into a place of worship different than their own would be encouraged by the commonality, especially the bond of family evident there. Despite all that had happened to them, their lives were moving forward, and the Temple provided a refuge for that to happen. Their services were very much a celebration of their faith, and as the families came together at the Temple, it seemed like a safe place again.

Security had been ramped up since August 5. A security guard was now stationed inside the main doors of the Temple. That aspect of Temple life would be forever different, the openness of the building now restricted by the realities of a recent mass shooting. Once into the building and past the security guard, the only reminder of the shooting was a single bullet hole on the right side of the doorframe of the prayer hall, left by the members to mark the significance of the event in their history.

After we greeted everyone, we were led into the prayer hall, a very large, open room where the Temple members celebrate their faith each day. The music of the *tabla* and *raja* alongside the reading and singing of their sacred scriptures fills the space. Inside the hall, women sit to the left, men to the right, the altar front and center at the end of the room. Here, Sikhs bow upon entering, a sign of respect for the *Guru Granth Sahib*, the holy book of devotional hymns considered the lasting *guru* or teacher. During the service, the *Granth* is gently fanned by a member of the Temple. On this visit, a *granthi,* a Sikh ceremonial reader or singer, sang the hymns. The words were projected onto a large screen left of the altar, the text in *Punjabi* with an occasional translation to English, a concession for visitors, and those members who don't speak *Punjabi.*

It wasn't widely known, but in the first few moments after Page was killed, a member of the Temple had rushed back inside to secure the *Granth*. They made sure that it was kept secure and not mishandled or misplaced in the aftermath and chaos of the shooting. That act had done a lot to soothe the fears of the other members of the Temple.

In the prayer hall, nearly all members sit on the floor on large white sheets placed over the carpet. The only chairs are set up along the back wall for the elderly or those with physical ailments. As the service ended, children wandered through the crowd, often engaging with family members or playing impromptu games of hide and seek. Children will always be children, Sikh or otherwise.

At the conclusion of the service, Dr. Kalwant Dhaliwal, the newly elected President of the Sikh Temple of Wisconsin, introduced us to the members and thanked us for coming. He then invited us to share their post-service meal in the *langar* hall, just adjacent to the prayer hall. It was another large room where Page had fired many rounds during the terror-filled moments when he moved through the Temple, looking for targets. Many of the survivors had been in the kitchen area as he began firing that day. They had sought refuge hiding in the pantry, scrambling to get out of his line of sight.

As special guests, we were seated in tables at the end of the room; typically the members of the Temple sit side by side on the floor on long carpets rolled out just for the *langar* meal. The dining room takes on a life of its own filled with the noise of many conversations and food preparation. In the kitchen, the women mixed *atta dough* for the flat bread called *roti,* fried on gas stoves. It accompanied the rice and vegetables of the day's meal. Spicy curry dishes, white rice, and lentil-based recipes are the staple of the *langar* menu. My wife Kathy, who doesn't appreciate spicy foods as I do, noticed that even the simple lettuce salad served that day had a peppery taste to it. At the Sikh Temple of Wisconsin, the meal is served on disposable Styrofoam trays with plastic spoons, a nod to ease of cleanup given the large number of people served each week. In many other *gurdwaras*, the meal is served on steel plates. *Langar* is an established practice in all *gurdwaras* in India, the U.S. and around the world. Any visitor can walk into a Sikh *gurdwara* for a free vegetarian meal as this practice represents a core tenet of the Sikh faith: *Seva*, or sacred service.

The *langar* meal, like any gathering, also offers an opportunity for talk. That day was filled with conversation about the recent visit by First Lady Michelle Obama on August 23, just a few weeks after the shooting. Dr. Dhaliwal and I had met with her at Oak Creek High School on the previous Friday. In an incredible window into what life for the President and his family is like, Dr. Dhaliwal and I met her in an interior hallway of the high school. The building was cleared of anyone else, except for a few selected media representatives, and surrounded by local law enforcement and the Secret Service. As we moved to a classroom, we sat down at a small table, three people of completely different backgrounds brought together by tragedy and a shared belief that we needed to heal the country.

The nation had just suffered through mass shootings in Aurora and Oak Creek, barely two weeks apart. That December, we would be reeling from the shock of Newtown, and the Sandy Hook elementary shootings. The Temple, an apolitical body, has members who have very strong political beliefs on the right and left. As we talked, the issue of gun violence and the role of the government in that relationship was front and center.

I heard the phrase "too many guns" many times that day. It was difficult to balance my belief in the strength of the 2nd Amendment with the harsh reality that in this building, lives were cut short and futures changed by guns legally obtained but used in such a brutal fashion. I would personally battle with that balance many times in the coming months, and I listened closely to their comments on that Sunday as they struggled to make sense out of it all.

On that day, many members of the Temple approached me. Some I had never met before, and who thanked me for my service to their community and for coming to visit.

It was an easy decision to come to the Temple. This community had become part of my life now after spending the greater part of the last three weeks talking about them, learning their stories, sharing their pain. The visit offered the chance to learn about life inside the Temple. I saw not only where it happened but also who it happened to. As an elected official, you are often given access to information and people's lives that you typically would only see or hear about on your local news. As the mayor of Oak Creek, the scene of one of the most violent attacks in the history of our country, I was now bonded with this community, who I knew so little about before, in a profound way.

I joked that day that I was becoming part of their family and made the comment that I had spent more time with them than I had with my two daughters and my wife. I had been to Temple more recently than I had been to my own Catholic church, a faith I still struggle to fully embrace.

As we finished our meal and left the Temple, I felt a strong connection with the members, sharing long hugs with many of them as we walked through the entryway, encouraged by their brightened faces and smiles. Some calm had returned here, bonds were being made, phone numbers exchanged with the promise of future conversations. Kathy and I drove back down the hill, silently past the places where the violence had happened, now just parking spots, no physical evidence of the act, or the hatred that had inspired it.

I would return here many times over the course of the next year, sharing afternoon *chai* and *langar* meals, but none of those trips had the impact of that first long visit. I had filled in some of the gaps in my knowledge about the shooting and could put it in physical context. Now perhaps I could begin to start to understand what role I could play in the future, and how our city could help shape a national conversation about violence. It would take me all the way to the nation's capitol and the White House, and despite its roots in this violent act, it was a discussion I was willing to have.

One Thousand Paper Cranes

Just over a month after the Temple shooting I walked into my office at City Hall and a saw small box sitting on my desk, not unusual given the volume of well wishes and gifts which had flooded into our building since August 5. It was shipped from Sacramento, California, home to a significant Sikh population, one of the largest in the United States.

The box was from Ms. Tera Carter, a teacher and Director of Student Activities at Norwood Junior High School. As I picked it up, I was surprised at how light it was. I noticed that it was addressed to me, not to Murphy or the police department, who were receiving the bulk of the correspondence. As I opened the box, it was apparent why it was so light. The box was filled with about 1,000 origami cranes, which popped out in spectacular fashion, spilling out across my desk. They had to have been carefully stuffed in her classroom back in Sacramento, and now they expended the stored energy of a cross-country trip at maximum compression in between California and Wisconsin.

The tradition of origami cranes is based on Japanese folklore, which suggests a gesture of peace or love. Ms. Carter explained in a letter that her class had just read *Sadako and the Thousand Paper Cranes*, a non-fiction

96

children's book, telling the story of a young Hiroshima survivor. They were inspired to construct them to show their support for the Sikh community in Oak Creek. The cranes, delicately folded from brightly colored paper, were a welcome surprise. As I showed them to the City Hall staff, I left a trail of color throughout the building, as many of the staff wanted one for their own desks.

Some of the cranes were placed in a growing collection of cards and letters in the main display case, across from the Clerk's counter at City Hall. I had wanted to share the correspondence from the White House, embassies around the world, and elected officials with our residents who were affected enough by the shooting to also take the time to hand-write letters of support or sympathy. As residents came into City Hall in the days and weeks after the shooting, many stopped by the display case to take the time to read them, and I frequently would spend some time each day talking to them, and providing whatever reassurance I could that things would get better.

Ms. Carter's letter asked me to share the cranes with the community in any manner that would help, and I immediately thought of an upcoming fundraiser for Murphy, which would be held at our local community center. Since the shooting Murphy had received thousands of dollars in donations from organizations around the world, and Chief Edwards had told me that it was pretty clear that he would never have to worry about his finances again, certainly reassuring news to his family, who had already suffered so much. I had also made arrangements for Murphy and all of the first responders to receive whatever medical or counseling help they needed, without regard to medical deductibles or limitations of their health coverage. I thought it was important to make sure that our fire and police staff was afforded every possible measure of assistance, given the impact of what they had been through both on August 5 and in the days after. Many of them had seen the aftermath of the shooting close-up and taking care of whatever they needed in the way of counseling, or medical attention was critical to their recovery as well.

At the same time we had been working on a fundraiser for Murphy, I had been contacted by Jasjit Singh of SALDEF asking if I would be willing to come out to their national gala in Washington D.C. and speak about what happened in Oak Creek and our city's response to the shooting. I had gotten to know Jasjit in the short time he had spent in our city during that first week after the shooting, offering the wisdom and guidance of the Sikh community to those of us who still knew so little about Sikhism and the people who practiced it. He offered me a chance to speak at the gala, along with Amardeep Kaleka, son of the slain Temple leader, and James Santelle, the U.S. Attorney from Milwaukee, highlighting key elements of the shooting from the perspectives of family, community and law enforcement. It would be one of the largest crowds I had ever spoken in front of, not counting the worldwide television coverage of our press conference, and I was certainly becoming aware of how Oak Creek was being viewed nationally. It was important to me that the story of the victims and the actions of our heroic police officers be told, and the opportunity to speak in front of a crowd of 500 assembled Sikhs, media and honored guests would be a chance to tell that story to the group most affected.

I had been to Washington D.C. many times before, having taken management classes there in the early 2000s for my previous job with the Nielsen Company, a media research firm best known for the television ratings. I loved the history and the architecture of the nation's capital. It was a quick, two-hour flight from Milwaukee, easy to get to for the weekend gala on October 6, 2012.

SALDEF is the oldest Sikh civil rights organization in the United States, and their annual national gala is a night devoted to honoring leaders in their community and others who serve the Sikh community through their public service. SALDEF and the Sikh Coalition had been invaluable to me in their service and insight on the ground in Oak Creek in the days immediately after the shooting. The 2012 gala was dedicated to the lives lost in Oak Creek. As one of the featured speakers at the gala, just two months after the shooting, I was honored to be there and my speech echoed the thoughts of our local Sikh community, and the role I believe we could play in laying out a path to reducing violence in our society. I had written the speech the day before at my desk in my office at home, searching for themes that would strike a chord with the audience. I also wanted to reach the general public, which was becoming increasingly restless with the perception that nothing could be done to halt the recent wave of mass shootings.

As I waited to speak that night, I anxiously felt for the folded copy of my speech in the inside pocket of my suit coat, and the folded origami crane I had also brought with me. It would be reassuring to have a prop, and as I walked to the podium, my nervousness relaxed. I carefully unfolded my speech, and placed that single orange crane next to it. The words came out, growing stronger with the message of hope and opportunity that the last two months had given me. Here are my comments from that night:

> *It is a great pleasure for me to be here tonight representing the City of Oak Creek, a city of 35,000 people, a suburb of Milwaukee, located on the shores of Lake Michigan.*

> *I want to share the news with you that Lt. Brian*

Murphy is doing well, continuing to recover quickly from his injuries, and his spirit and his enthusiasm have remained high. Brian was honored last week by the National Police Association and he is truly a hero. When I received a phone call from our chief on that Sunday morning August 5, a clear, sunny day in Wisconsin, I never imagined that our community would be impacted in this way, and that so many lives would be affected, those of our local gurdwara members, our fire and police first responders, and for all of us, who live our lives, day to day, but never think something like this could happen in our city.

But what this event has also shown me there is good in our society. The kindness and support of all of our citizens, those in Wisconsin, the rest of the country, and the world, have been nothing short of amazing, and this support continues to this day. At City Hall I received an outpouring of letters, emails, and voice-mails since August 5. They all deliver the same message...WE STAND WITH YOU!

Here is one of those messages:

"I am proud of our city, Oak Creek, I am proud to be a citizen of a city that responded overwhelmingly with compassion and openness to a group of

people that we are not entirely familiar with. I hope we continue to build bridges with ALL people in our city who look, sound, or pray in ways that are not familiar to us. We have a great opportunity to learn and grow, and to build more bridges in our future."

That was from one of our residents, a woman who felt strongly enough to say she was willing to help move the dialogue from TRAGEDY to HEALING to CHANGE.

This is the message I go forward with tonight and where I will focus my attention and my efforts.

At a vigil on the Tuesday following the shooting, we came together as a community, thousands of us, praying together, honoring the victims, calming and reassuring each other, unconcerned about what was different about us, focusing instead on what we shared.

Since that day we have held many events including fundraisers, interfaith gatherings, and community discussions. This past Saturday, our local high school students, with help from our friends at the Sikh Temple, planted a diversity prairie garden in front of the high school, honoring our shared experiences, and showing us all what diversity is really about- an appreciation that celebrating our differences, knowing that those things that make us different- enrich all of our lives.

What we do from this point on can shift the attention away from a violent act of extreme hate to a community response that says simply . . . We will not let this define us, and we will work together as one to stop it.

We are proud to stand shoulder to shoulder with the members of our local Sikh community and Sikhs worldwide.

I'm often asked, "What can I do to stop this from happening somewhere else?" Here is how I respond. As an individual, communicate with cultures and groups that are different than your own, get to know your neighbors, and engage in a dialogue that promotes and encourages cultural acceptance. Having spent the last two months doing just that, I can tell you that it has changed me, not only as an elected official, but as a citizen.

Encourage your elected officials to stand up against discrimination, and to actively participate in opening the avenues of understanding for all people at all levels of our government.

To our government – recognize and acknowledge the Sikh community as a statistic, so that hate crimes against them can be counted and included in the tracking of these acts against our own citizens, within our own borders. Members of the Sikh community deserve the dignity of being counted.

Examine the process that creates a culture and an environment of hate and work towards reducing that by all legal means necessary. We are a country of freedoms, but those freedoms should never include the targeting and persecution of one group based on nothing more than a blind perception that is fundamentally wrong.

Last week I received a box in my office at City Hall. When I opened it, I saw that it was filled with 1000 origami cranes, folded by middle school students from Sacramento, California. Here is one of those cranes, which were made to celebrate the international day of peace. Those students give me hope and encourage me to work harder every day, and I carry this small token to remind me of the support we have all around us. Thanks again to all of you for the kindness you have shown me. I will continue to work toward peace, and I ask all of you to join me in those efforts.

When I spoke those words that night, I felt an even greater bond with the Sikh community and their reaction to my speech reinforced that belief. They applauded loudly when I talked about the efforts to include Sikhs in national crime statistics and gave me a very warm welcome throughout the evening. Many in the audience came up after the gala and shared stories of their lives in America, and how they had succeeded in a country that had seen them as different, or in the context of September 11, 2001, threatening. I had met one of the evening's honorees at a faith event in Milwaukee a week after the shooting. Valarie Kaur, a striking Sikh American woman with an intense passion for community service, has worked tirelessly for Sikh-Americans and the advocacy of civil rights through her films and campaigns, including through *Groundswell,* an initiative of Auburn Seminary she founded in 2011.

Valarie had been in Oak Creek in the days and weeks after the Oak Creek tragedy, one of several national Sikh advocates who helped the community organize and tell their story to the nation. Her husband Sharat Raju, also a filmmaker, would eventually play a larger role in the telling of the story of Oak Creek and the attack in 2012, this time with a short film that went viral on the one year anniversary of the shooting. Oak Creek and its Sikh community had an advocate on a national stage now, and the national conversation would soon shift to gun control and the rights of Sikhs to be treated as equals, even in the eyes of the FBI.

Law enforcement photo of
Wade Michael Page

Police Chief John Edwards

Sikh Temple of Wisconsin

Outside the Sikh Temple of Wisconsin, Afternoon, August 5, 2012

Satellite trucks set up across the street from the Sikh Temple

Members of the Overpass Light Brigade at the Community
Vigil on August 7, 2012

Lt. Brian Murphy with members of the Sikh Temple of Wisconsin

Community Vigil held in Miller Park on August 7, 2012

Lt. Brian Murphy accepting his Badge of Bravery award

Officer Sam Lenda receiving the Badge of Bravery award

Gurvinder with Lt. Brian Murphy and Officer Sam Lenda

Chief John Edwards, Lt. Brian Murphy and visiting
police officers from Toronto, Canada

Paper cranes sent by students from Tera Carter's class
to Oak Creek City Hall

Meeting with Wisconsin Congressman Paul Ryan at National Night Out

Flyer from the Oak Creek premiere of *Waking in Oak Creek*

Pardeep Kaleka and Arno Michaelis

US Conference of Mayors meeting in Washington D.C. from left to right,
Mayor Steve Hogan, Mayor Ron Rordam, Mayor Stephen Scaffidi,
and Mayor Jonathan Rothschild

Starting line of the inaugural *Chardi Kala 6k* in August, 2013

Flags flying at half-mast at National Night Out to honor the
victims of the Sikh Temple Shooting.

Sam Lenda – "I saw evil in that parking lot"

The night before August 5, 2012, Sam Lenda had been at home reading the book *Lone Survivor* by Marcus Luttrell. Luttrell's book documented his service as a Navy Seal in Afghanistan, and the harrowing mission in 2005 that only he survived. The book, and the later film starring Mark Wahlberg, is a testament to the will to survive and courage under fire. Lenda didn't know it that night, but he would need all of his skills and courage the next morning. One of the chapters in the book is titled *Murphy's Ridge,* a remarkable coincidence given he would driving to the aid of one of his fellow officers, Murphy, and to a gun battle of his own.

Lenda, a 33-year veteran of the Oak Creek police department at the time of the shooting, did something on the morning of August 5 that he had never done in his long, distinguished career. He forgot his SWAT gear, which he typically stored in the trunk of his squad car when he got to work. His shift on August 5, 2012 started at 7:00 a.m. and he had been dispatched almost immediately to a call at a hotel on the northwest side of the city, a fight between two people in the parking lot. When he arrived there, he quickly received the dispatcher calls for a shooting at the Sikh Temple. Driving east on College Avenue, before making the turn south onto Howell Avenue just north of the Temple, he drove his squad car over the median and up the long driveway of the Temple.

He looked for the lights of Murphy's squad car, and didn't see them. Almost immediately, he noticed an individual dressed in military style clothing who approached him in a threatening manner, which caused Lenda to pull his squad back down the driveway. He unlocked the squad rifle, an AR-15, which was located between the seats in the squad car and took a defensive position behind the door, something his years of SWAT training had taught him. Lenda had not only trained and been involved in tactical situations but was considered a marksman throughout his long career. He also served as a police instructor at our local technical college.

As he noticed Wade Michael Page moving toward him, Lenda shouted, "drop your weapon" twice. As Page fired, his bullet shattered the windshield of the squad car and sprayed glass across Lenda's face. At that point, Lenda fired six shots at Page, eventually hitting him in the abdomen and knocking him down. Page then took his own weapon and fired a fatal shot into his head. Lenda quickly drove up to Page's body, kicked his gun away, and immediately began looking for Murphy, loudly shouting "where's Murphy" to his fellow officers. He found Murphy lying behind a vehicle, bleeding from multiple gunshot wounds, and called in the ambulances to get him to the hospital. His quick action not only increased Murphy's

survival chances, but also prevented an even greater loss
of life at the Temple.

For a month after the shooting, City Attorney Larry Haskin,
Police Chief John Edwards, and I had argued that the dash
cam video of the incident on August 5 should be released.
Haskin made the case that it not only showed the public
what had happened, but also demonstrated the
outstanding police work done by our department on that
day. The first hurdle was the clearing of the officers'
conduct by Milwaukee District Attorney John Chisholm.
This was routine in any officer-involved shooting, but it
was significant in that Lenda couldn't go back to work until
he was cleared, something he wanted to do. Teresa
Carlson, Special Agent in Charge of Milwaukee's FBI
division, had argued against the release, citing an open
investigation. At several meetings on the subject at the
Oak Creek police station, Haskin forcefully made the case
that because the video belonged to the City of Oak Creek
and that once the officer's conduct had been cleared, the
investigation would not be impacted by the release of
the video.

In the first week of September 2012, Chisholm exonerated
the officers and cleared the way for the public release of
the dash cam video. On September 10, in the same
courtroom where the initial press conference was held the
day after the shooting, District Attorney Chisholm made

the comments we had been waiting to hear, and publicly cleared both officers.

"There is no question in my mind that Murphy's intervention prevented Page from continuing this rampage" Chisholm added, noting that because of Murphy and Lenda's actions many lives were probably saved that day.

Once again, I stepped up to the microphone in front of a courtroom full of local and national press, this time to commend the work of the department and its officers. Now, more than a month after the shooting, I was much more confident in my delivery and the emotion of the events had quieted down considerably. My comments were brief:

> As has been stated, we are very proud of the work done by the Oak Creek police officers and all the emergency responders on August 5. I echo the comments of the district attorney and we send our support and prayers to the victims, their families and the community at large as they cope with the tragic events of that day.
>
> As you view this video, I think you'll agree that our police officers acted in a professional and heroic manner, and most likely prevented the loss of

*addition lives. Both Chief Edwards and one of the
initial responding officers Sam Lenda are here to
talk about the video you'll see, and the events of
that day.*

For the next hour, Chief Edwards and Officer Lenda led the
assembled media through a second by second review of
the edited video, a compilation of dash cam footage from
both Murphy and Lenda's squad cars. We hired a
Milwaukee company, Mueller Communications, to assist
us on the logistics of a national release of the video, and
they prepared us not only for the technical requirements
of the release, but also in the preparation of our officers. It
was significant that the officer directly involved in the
event was narrating the video, and this was a testament to
Lenda's experience and training, but also to his ability to
directly relate what he did on that day to what the video
showed. Lenda has done many presentations using the
video since and he has a remarkable ability to translate the
events from not only a technical police perspective, but
also to talk about what he personally experienced as the
events unfolded.

On May 17, 2013, Lenda and Murphy were honored as the
co-recipients of the Oak Creek Citizens of the Year award,
given to individuals for leadership and community
engagement. In his acceptance speech Lenda said "I
confronted evil in that parking lot" and he told the

audience that he could not let Page get out of that parking lot or back into the Temple, fearing that many more lives would have been lost. He talked about his actions on August 5 and his role in the response on that Sunday morning. As was typical of Lenda, he deflected any talk of heroism or bravery, calling his work as a police officer just part of doing his job. For those of us who know Lenda, it's not surprising that he feels this way. In his career, he has had thousands of interactions with individuals and has been directly involved in nearly every type of police situation possible, including many tactical events.

Typically, the highest-tenured officers on police department staffs are not usually the first line of defense for a department. In Oak Creek's case, we were lucky that two of our most well-trained and respected officers were on duty that day, both on patrol in the city. Lenda was just doing his job, fortunately for our community it was at the highest level possible.

Lenda received the most prestigious honor for a police officer, the Congressional Badge of Bravery, along with Murphy on Wednesday, August 6, 2014 at the Oak Creek Community Center. The two officers, with their families in attendance, accepted the awards from U.S. Senator Ron Johnson and Congressman Paul Ryan. Each thanked the other officer for what they had done that day. Extraordinary circumstances had brought them to the

121

Temple that morning on the fifth of August in 2012. Two of the most tenured officers in the department responded with decades of experiences to guide their actions, and each put their own safety at risk to save the lives of others. Their actions defined the words *to protect and serve* and certainly made the telling of our story that much easier.

A Trip to the White House

Just after New Year's, in the first few days of January 2013, I was walking into a local Woodman's grocery store with my wife Kathy when my phone began ringing, the display showing *blocked* again. This time I picked it up. On the phone was Elias Alcantara, staff assistant for the Department of Intergovernmental Affairs at the White House, asking if I would be interested in coming to the White House to participate in the President's conference on gun violence. Alcantara serves as the liaison between the federal government and local municipalities, and we had exchanged emails previously on several issues, including the federal budget negotiations and the August visit to Oak Creek by the First Lady.

The White House had invited several local leaders to the event at the White House including Selectman Pat Llondra of Newton, Connecticut, the scene of the Sandy Hook elementary school shooting, and Ron Rordam from Blacksburg, Virginia, the scene of the Virginia Tech Shootings. I had sent an email to Llondra shortly after December 14, offering my support and prayers as she struggled through the days after the shooting in Newtown. She had never gotten back to me, not that I expected her to take the time. I was looking forward to meeting both of these local leaders, who had served their communities so well during the toughest time possible. The public has an

123

expectation that leaders have a road map on how to deal with tragedy in their cities, but other than a basic emergency preparedness plan, most of us don't get much in the way of guidance on how to deal with a mass shooting. Because events like this are still relatively rare, although the Aurora-Oak Creek-Newton shootings in rapid succession seemed to contradict that, it would be unreasonable to expect that every scenario could be anticipated or trained for.

I had been to Washington, D.C. just a few months earlier for the SALDEF Gala, and despite making that recent trip, I was more than happy to travel again for the opportunity to meet the President in person. As someone who had seen the White House from beyond the gates numerous times, it would be exciting to be on the inside of one of the most famous buildings in the world. This trip would be much different. I would be sitting in the audience of a White House press conference on gun violence prevention. In the eyes of some, potentially being used as a pawn to make the case for a significant change in the access and sale of assault weapons, and in a ramping-up of the background check process.

The discussion of gun control and gun violence had ramped up since the shooting in Oak Creek, followed up by the tragic shooting in Newtown, Connecticut in December, where 26 children, teachers and staff had been killed in horrific fashion by a young man with serious mental health issues. I had also recently signed on with the group *Mayors Against Illegal Guns*. I was already being confronted by angry gun-rights groups who felt that any discussion of increased background checks, or limiting the access to assault weapons was somehow an unconstitutional infringement on their 2nd Amendment gun rights. As a gun owner and a hunter, I had no reservation signing and endorsing some of the common-sense measures requested by MAIG. The two that made the most sense to me were universal background checks for all gun sales, and efforts to increase the penalties for gun trafficking. I was comfortable with restrictions that balanced the rights of the individual with the safety and security of the public. As a country, we had already done that. In my opinion, background checks, restrictions on the possession of weapons inside public buildings, airports, and public stadiums, properly walked the line between rights and responsibility, the true measure of the effectiveness of public policy.

This trip would be perfectly timed. I was already committed to attending the U.S. Conference of Mayor's annual winter meeting in Washington, D.C. The White House visit was scheduled for the day before. It would involve a change to my flight, but MAIG had arranged for several meetings in the Capital with members of Congress, asking them to support the proposed legislation. I had made it clear early on that I didn't support everything in MAIG's checklist for common-sense gun reform, but with overwhelming public support of increased and effective background checks, I thought it was important that one of the local leaders in a city that was impacted by a mass shooting be part of the discussion.

I can still remember my initial reaction to the Newtown shootings. On Friday, December 14, I was driving to western Wisconsin, on my way to meet up with some friends for a guys weekend, which for me meant smoking cigars, drinking brandy Manhattans, and enjoying my first weekend away since the Temple shooting. As I drove west on Interstate 94 out of Milwaukee, a radio report came on mid-morning with the news that a gunman had entered an elementary school with shots fired in Connecticut. That report was quickly followed up by a phone call from the news producer of one of the local radio stations asking me for my comments on the shooting. Just as the mayors of cities impacted by mass shootings were quickly connected by tragedy, I was linked to other shootings by the local media, who often called me now to comment on current events, especially when they involved guns. I was honest with them. When I heard the story, I literally pounded my steering wheel in anger. Just a few months after the Aurora and Oak Creek shootings, here we were again. How could someone kill innocent children in an elementary school, children who had done nothing wrong? They were

126

brutally gunned down inside their classrooms, naive to whatever issue was on the gunman's mind. My rage was profound. As I tried to calm myself, the realization that it was children who were killed changed the discussion in my mind. Clearly, we had crossed a line in this country. Was there no safe zone, no place immune from violence?

When I went to Washington a few weeks later, I went with a purpose, advocating for the victims of the Temple shooting. My resolve deepened after Newton, and I was looking forward to the chance to interact with the President and the Vice President in the White House, not the typical day in the life of a small city mayor. Because I had to preside over a late night Common Council meeting the evening before my White House trip, I decided to leave immediately after the meeting, making the drive to Chicago in a little over an hour. Camped out in a hotel room less than five minutes from O'Hare airport in Chicago, I carefully laid out my suit for the next day on the couch. With a 3:30 a.m. wakeup, I wanted to be sure that I was ready to go. I got a hotel wakeup call and set the alarm on my phone. The last thing I wanted to do was to miss the opportunity of a lifetime because I overslept and missed my flight to Washington.

As my flight left Chicago and I flew east toward Washington, the sun was coming up, providing a spectacular view from my window seat on the plane, a brilliant array of colors announcing the arrival of the day. I wasn't sure what to expect and was slightly nervous, given where I was going. I was honored to be invited to the White House, regardless of the reason why, and would bring with me a letter from the Temple victim's families, carrying it right to the President.

Arriving in Washington in plenty of time for my short cab ride to the White House, I decided to take the cab to my hotel instead, dropping off my bags and checking in at the Capital Hilton, site of the U.S. Mayor's conference. It was raining that morning so I borrowed a hotel umbrella and slowly walked south down 16th Street NW, the White House just a few blocks away. It was an inspiring site, even on a gloomy day, the whitewashed sandstone facade looming ahead, the home to the President and the First-family, and the scene of so much history and significance. One of the characteristics of Washington that always stands out when I visit is the scale and architecture of the buildings, unlike any other place in our country. *Grand* things happening in *grand* buildings.

I was early, and because I was instructed to check in at the guard shack on West Executive Avenue at 11:00 a.m., I camped out in the lobby of the Federal Deposit Insurance building a block away. I checked out the historical displays and probably gave the security guards a reason to wonder why I was lingering in their lobby. As 11:00 a.m. arrived, I walked to the White House guard shack, showed my ID, and went through the first of several checkpoints on the way to the press conference, my heart rate more than likely elevated given the significance of where I was.

Once inside, I went through a more detailed check, emptying my pockets and wanded by White House security before signing in at another final checkpoint. A few minutes later, I was met by a young member of the White House staff who escorted me through the building to the South Court Auditorium, where the press conference would be held. It's impossible not to feel the history when you're walking through the White House. I took notice of the wall hangings and fixtures, even the detailed, ornate wood moldings as I passed through the hallways leading into the auditorium.

It was half full as I entered, and I had to ask another member of the staff where to sit, not wanting to step on any toes during my first visit to the White House. They seated me to the left, about six rows back of the podium positioned on the low stage at the front of the room. It was close enough, but far enough back to take in the rest of the audience and hear the buzz in the room roughly 40 minutes before the start of the press conference. I had seen this room on television many times, the traditional blue drapery hanging floor to ceiling at the rear of the stage, a perfect backdrop for a presidential address.

As the other guests arrived, I noticed that I was seated next to Selectwoman Llondra and Mayor Rordam, with Philadelphia Mayor Michael Nutter to my left, then president of the U.S. Conference of Mayors. President Obama would mention Oak Creek, Newton, and Blacksburg in his remarks. Each of us represented cities that had been through tremendous tragedy and had pushed our respective cities through adversity. Here we sat together in the audience for what many thought would be a signature speech of President Obama's second term. The room slowly filled up. I noticed Reverend Al Sharpton, members of the media in the back of the room, and a mix of Senators and Congressmen scattered throughout the first few rows.

Selectwoman Llondra, a petite, former schoolteacher was only 33 days removed from the Newtown shooting, but was cheery and optimistic in our brief conversation as we sat down, waiting for the Vice President to make his introductory remarks. Shared adversity brought us together in Washington, waiting for words of wisdom on a national stage from the leader of the country.

Seated on the right side of the stage were four children who had written letters to the President after the Newtown shootings, and they would become targets themselves as gun rights groups later called their appearance staged, and the President's use of them at the press conference inappropriate. Whatever anyone's opinion on gun violence, the fact that these children had written to the President and expressed their fears about what they had seen and heard in Newtown made me realize that there was genuine concern across the country about the threat of violence, and that something needed to be done. What that something was, clearly, was going to take center stage in this upcoming national discussion.

Watching the Vice President and President confidently stride onto the stage in that auditorium was something I never thought I would witness in person. To see that in the White House was even more impressive and surreal. My mind quickly flashed through the events in my life since August 5, and everything I had seen since. In the space of a few months, I had now spoken with the President, First Lady, and the Vice President, each in the context of what had happened in Oak Creek and now part of a broader discussion on gun violence. I was connected to the story, because I was the Mayor of Oak Creek, but I was also committed to doing something about the problem that seemed to be consuming not only our national attention, but also many innocent lives in the process, including 20 first-graders from Sandy Hook Elementary.

Vice President Biden led off the press conference, recognizing the parents of Grace McDonald, one of the children killed in Newtown, seated in the front row. As he

spoke, the room was silent, only a few quiet sniffles
marking the gravity of what had happened a month
earlier. Biden talked about his long political career and his
work in the area of gun violence during his service in the
Senate, recalling that he sponsored what was the last
significant legislation related to guns. At one point, he
cited a line from a Voltaire poem, saying, "We cannot let
perfect be the enemy of good." He said he had never seen
the nation as shaken as they were at this moment. The
Vice President's remarks on January 16, 2013 were
contextual, setting the table for a more specific ask from
the President to follow. If Biden's words provided the
historical significance of the day, the President's remarks
looked to the immediate future, aimed at a direct target,
the impact of guns in the daily life of every American.

President Obama began by acknowledging the four
children seated on stage to his left in his opening remarks,
asking them each to wave to the audience as he said their
name. He informed us that immediately after he was done
speaking, he would sign 23 executive orders. It was a long
list and impacted background checks, the tracking of guns
used in criminal investigations, expanded the
government's research into gun violence, and adding some
flexibility for local municipalities and school districts to use
grant funding to improve public safety. While anything the
President would do in the way of gun violence would upset
at least half the population, it was his remarks about

Congress that would be the most controversial. These proposals would generate almost immediate attacks from the National Rifle Association, who promised to bitterly oppose any measure even distantly related to gun control, despite overwhelming support on some of the proposals from their own members.

As I watched the President speak, it was interesting to note his demeanor in his presentation, the ease with which he addressed the assembled group, the affection he had shown toward the children, and the heartfelt sincerity he used when speaking directly to the victims' families. Like most great public speakers, he understood the link between words and their delivery, and this connection was something that separated him from most public officials. Despite not voting for him in the 2008 Presidential election, I was honored to be at the White House that day.

Immediately after the President signed the executive orders, Mayor Nutter, Rordam, and myself, along with Selectwoman Llondra, were ushered into an adjacent room off to the side of the stage. Vice President Biden spent about 15 minutes with us, telling us about his work on the issues of gun violence and his expectations for the proposed legislation. The Vice President was extremely passionate and personal in his conversation, engaging each of us directly, at one point putting his hand on my shoulder and addressing me as Mayor. He urged us to go back to our communities and make the case for the measures laid out that day. I told my wife Kathy later that day on the phone that speaking with the Vice President was like having a conversation at the corner bar. His passionate delivery, hands-on with whomever he was speaking to, gave him a likability that put me and everyone else in the room at ease. He was the ultimate good guy, and easy to talk to, two traits I admired about him.

When the President arrived in the room, signaled first by the arrival of an official White House photographer, the meeting immediately took on a more serious and official tone. In a room roughly the size of my kitchen at home, we now had the President of the United States, the Vice President and a select group of local leaders who had suffered the effects of gun violence first-hand in their respective cities. It was in this room that I had the opportunity to thank the President personally for the phone call he made to me in the evening of August 5, 2012. I was actually older than the President, who was born in 1961, but when standing face to face with him, it was honestly more like speaking to my father. Respect for the position and appreciation for the difficulties of the job made it easy to look up to the President, despite our different political affiliations. As we gathered together to take a group picture, I thought about the significance of this moment, not only in my life, but also in the story of Oak Creek, and how we had responded after the shooting.

We had now come all the way to Washington, D.C. and the White House, but there was still work to do at home, and in Congress, for the rights and equal treatment of Sikh Americans. I had made that promise to them months ago.

As I slowly walked back to my hotel after the meeting, I noticed the rain had stopped sometime during my visit. The pavement was still wet. I felt a rush of excitement and newfound resolve to push forward. There was no clear path for changing the cycle of violence in the country, but I was even more committed to looking for an answer.

Wade Michael Page

In the days, weeks, and months since August 5, 2012, I've met thousands of people, from residents and political leaders to the families of the victims of the Sikh Temple shooting. Often those conversations include a basic question. Why did Wade Michael Page choose the Sikh Temple of Wisconsin?

Trying to assign a motive to a perpetrator who is dead, unless he's left a manifesto or a digital trail of emails explaining his actions, is next to impossible. What we have learned about Page after the shooting may provide some background on what his motivation might have been on August 5. From the FBI reports written about him, I learned that he was born in Colorado in 1971. He served in the U.S. Army from 1992 to 1998, and was discharged for issues related to alcohol. He had a relatively light criminal record that included an operating while intoxicated and reckless driving charge. Page joined the white supremacist movement in 2000 and was a member until 2012. During that time, he played in seven different white power bands and was a member of the virulent Hammerskins organization, considered to be the most organized white supremacist group in the U.S.

Page relocated to Cudahy, Wisconsin in 2011 and moved in with a woman named Misty, who was also associated with a white power group. Their relationship lasted just over six months, and ended when he broke up with her in June of 2012. His then ex-girlfriend revealed to Page's Hammerskins associates that he had previously dated a woman who was a minority, and this revelation ended Page's relationship with that group.

The timeline after June 2012 is even more specific. After he lost his job, Page spent most of his time watching white supremacist videos, drinking and playing video games, often for hours every day. In July, he pawned most of his possessions and purchased a handgun, along with three extended magazines. It was a legal purchase, which required a background check, one that he passed. On August 1, Page closed his storage locker and a day later, sold his Xbox gaming system. One day before the shooting, Page allegedly sold his computer, which was never located, shaved his head, and in what would be his last contact with the Hammerskins, mailed his member's patch and shirt back to the group in Illinois.

Little is known about how Page spent his last 24 hours. What is clear is that on August 5, just after 10:00 a.m., he drove his red truck up the long driveway off Howell Avenue and killed six members of the Temple. He injured several others including Murphy, before he ended his own life with a shot to his head in the parking lot.

Why Page chose the Sikh Temple of Wisconsin to carry out his rampage will never be known. He may have driven by the Temple in the past and made the connection in his mind to a minority group that his white supremacist dogma told him to hate. Perhaps Page had confronted a member of the Temple in the past and had an unresolved issue – although the interviews and law enforcement reports on the shooting indicate there were no previous contacts. Whatever happened before August 5 doesn't change the fact that Page drove the six miles from his residence in Cudahy and made his way to the Temple parking lot. Depending on the route he took that day, he drove by other places of worship, including two churches on Howell Avenue just north of the Temple. He made the conscious decision to drive by all of them and continue on to the Sikh Temple.

Regardless of Page's motive, the group he acted out on didn't respond in anger or with thoughts of revenge. After their initial shock subsided and the tremendous grief and sadness of what happened slowly began to wane, the collective feeling in the Temple community was to return to normalcy as soon as possible. Each day after the shooting we met with law enforcement and the Temple leadership, who asked when they would be able to get back in to the building. After the FBI completed their initial investigation and documentation of the crime scene, the Temple was turned back to the members on Thursday,

August 9. It immediately shifted back to a place where the families could come together, celebrate their faith, and begin to put their lives back together.

There was a significant amount of work to do inside the Temple when the members returned. Walls were painted, floors were mopped, and in some of the rooms, bullet holes were repaired. With the exception of one. On the right side of the doorframe leading into the prayer hall, a single bullet hole marked the tragedy. It is the only physical remnant of the shooting in the Temple.

When Wade Michael Page walked into the Sikh Temple of Wisconsin, he was armed to kill as many people as he could. His decision to engage Murphy also probably saved the lives of many other members of the Temple who were defenseless and trapped inside the building. Why he chose the Sikh Temple and not another church or group of people is a question whose answer may never be known. But the absence of motive doesn't dilute the reality that this was a hate crime committed by an individual with a history of allegiance to white supremacist organizations. If his intent was to kill people, he succeeded; although our first responding police officers probably reduced that number significantly. If Page intended to escalate the hatred toward immigrants and Americans who look and pray differently, he failed in our city. But nationally, since our shooting, attacks have continued against Sikh

Americans and the presence and impact of white supremacist organizations has not diminished. Awareness and understanding of Sikhs is a work in progress, and while our efforts locally have certainly helped, the country still struggles with the acceptance of new arrivals, despite hundreds of years of experience.

Kamal – "Losing your Mother"

Kamal Saini and his younger brother Harpreet both share the same goal: to graduate from college and work in law enforcement, in their minds, the ultimate example of *seva*, or service to the community. When their mother Paramjit Kaur was killed in the Sikh Temple shooting, their goals didn't change, nor did their drive to make sure that her life was not lived in vain.

A little more than a month after the death of their mother on September 19, 2012, in front of a U.S. Senate Subcommittee, Harpreet testified for the rights of Sikhs to be considered as a statistic in FBI tracking of hate crimes against religious groups. He was the first Sikh to testify in front of a congressional committee on civil rights and he dedicated his testimony to his mother.

I first met the young brothers in front of their mother's casket in the gymnasium at Oak Creek High School, on the Friday after the shooting. As I walked past the six caskets lined up across the north wall of the gymnasium, the grief and the tremendous sense of sadness that each of the family members had lived with since late in the day on August 5 was clear. The brothers faced the reality that their mother was gone. A woman who had devoted her life to her two sons and stressed the importance of getting an education, something they both were doing when she

141

was killed. Both brothers are looking to pursue careers in law enforcement, something Kamal Saini said his mother would have loved to see.

When I met with Kamal over a year after the shooting, he told me that he wanted to be a police officer even before his mother was killed. "The irony is that I wasn't able to help her," Kamal said. "I will never get used to the idea that when I am in the prayer hall, that is where she was killed. Every time I drive by or visit the Temple I remember her, and I never want to lose that."

Kamal and his brother are both Oak Creek High School graduates. Each came to the United States unable to speak English and it took them almost two years to be able to have a conversation with their classmates. Kamal credited his teachers and principal for their willingness to help them one on one and the English as a second language coursework designed to ease them into their new school.

When our conversation swung back to the shooting, Kamal reflected on what the loss of his mother had meant for him and his brother Harpreet. "She did everything for us, and probably spoiled us," he said. "Now we have responsibilities for each other, and the biggest change is that we have to do things for ourselves now." The two share an apartment, and Kamal, two years older than Harpreet, looks out for his younger brother who loves computers and video games.

Kamal has noticed the changes at the Temple since the shooting and the increase in the diversity of the people that stop to visit. He told me about a recent visit to the Temple where he saw people of three different races stop to leave flowers and share a *langar* meal. "I never saw that before," Kamal said. I've met him at the Temple on many of my visits there over the last year and it is a place where non-Sikhs can visit; some out of curiosity, others to pay their respects. Residents of Oak Creek and surrounding communities have often asked me about the Temple and whether they could stop at the Temple during their Sunday services. All Sikh *gurdwaras* are open to visitors, offering a meal in the *langar* hall for anyone who would like to share a meal with them. I've met many visitors during my trips to the Temple, often serving as an unofficial welcome guide, introducing them to the members of the Temple that I've come to know so well since August 5. Kamal has worked with other members of the Temple to develop relationships with non-Sikhs in Oak Creek and outside of the community in an outreach effort designed to improve interfaith relations.

As his Sikh faith had taught him, Kamal didn't think of violence as a response to the shooting. "I have no hate in my heart," he told me. "There was disbelief that it actually happened, but if my Mom was to die, she went as a martyr." Harpreet was motivated by his mother's death to stop cutting his hair, along with several other members of the Temple. The shooting inspired many of the members to recommit to their faith, and the two brothers saw the opportunity after the shooting to spread the word of their faith, but also to remember their mother. A woman who had spent her life celebrating her religion, praying in the Temple's main prayer hall as Wade Michael Page began his rampage.

The brothers continue to push forward on their goals to one-day serve as police officers. "I would love to be an Oak Creek police officer," Kamal told me. "Oak Creek has been so good to us, it would be a tremendous story."

How I got there

As the details of Wade Michael Page's story slowly emerged, I heard that he had been living on Holmes Avenue in Cudahy, Wisconsin, a city where I had grown up and spent most of my youth. Just a few houses down and across the street from the duplex where Page had lived was the home where my grandparents had settled in Cudahy when they came over from Sicily in the early 1900s. I had lived in Cudahy, a city just six miles from Oak Creek and also located along Lake Michigan, until I was a sophomore in high school. In 1974, my parents decided to move to Oak Creek — a move I wasn't very happy with at the time — and I graduated from Oak Creek High School in 1976.

I knew the area that Page lived in very well. My parents, my younger brother Bob, and many other relatives still lived there and the city had not changed much in the 30 years since I had called it home. Cudahy is dominated by two things: Patrick Cudahy, a meat plant famous for its smoked bacon and sausage founded in 1888 by the man who gave the city its name, and a beautiful stretch of park located along the Lake Michigan shoreline. It's a smaller city than Oak Creek in both geography and population, and known for its affordable single-family homes and duplexes arranged tightly together along narrow city streets.

Page had probably chosen Cudahy as a place to live because of its lower-cost housing, and he had nothing in common with the other residents of the city who are hard-working folks, many of whose families had lived in Cudahy for many generations. Skinheads were not a group they were used to seeing in their community, and his neighbors in Cudahy would probably have reacted in the same way most people do when they see someone wearing military-style clothing and adorned with racist tattoos and a shaved head; with aversion and suspicion.

After graduating from high school, I moved back to Cudahy, renting a three bedroom flat with two friends from Oak Creek, each of us enrolled at the University of Wisconsin-Milwaukee. I had moved out of my parents' home in Oak Creek to stretch my wings a bit, and the independence was definitely part of the growing up process for me. Unlike most college students today, I worked full-time at a grocery store at night while attending classes during the day and this early exposure to responsibility was something that I needed at that time, having expended only minimum effort during my high school years. I was a Mass Communications student at UWM focused on radio and television broadcasting, although I wasn't particularly drawn to any of the on-air aspects of that major. My education there probably put in place some basic media sensitivity; at least enough that I understood what the media was about, and how it

worked. In that sense, this training may have given me
some baseline ability to know what I was doing when I
stepped up in front of the microphones on August 5, 2012
to talk with the media about the shooting.

It was at UWM where I reconnected with my wife Kathy,
who had also gone to Oak Creek High School, but who I
only had spoken with a few times during those high-school
years. Toward the end of my time at UWM, she spent a
semester there and we began dating right around New
Year's of 1983, and were married in 1985. After I
graduated from college I applied at several companies in
my field of study and was hired by Nielsen Media
Research, now the Nielsen Company, to recruit sample
homes in their newly created national people-meter panel.
For me, it meant a relocation to San Francisco, so for
almost a year, I lived on my own in California, coming back
to Wisconsin for holidays and other family events. Kathy
eventually moved out to California with me, and we lived
there for two years before moving back to the Midwest.
Our two daughters, Katherine and Christina, were both
born outside of Wisconsin. Katherine in California and
Christina in Illinois, when we briefly lived just south of the
Wisconsin-Illinois border to be closer to our families.

For the next 28 years, I worked for the Nielsen Company in
a variety of positions, all with a communications and
management focus. I believe that these experiences gave

me some ability to speak effectively and to understand the importance of leadership as it relates to crisis management, budgeting, and probably most importantly, people. I've talked about my time with Nielsen and the number of conversations I had during those years in all kinds of situations, as the primary builder of my leadership skill-sets. I have to believe that any ability I have to deal with the stresses of running a city, or in the case of the Sikh Temple shooting, the ability to respond in a calm, professional manner is a result of the thousands of conversations I had during my time there.

Kathy and I had moved back to Oak Creek in 1993. With two small children, I didn't spend a lot of time focusing on city government or anything beyond our own family, but as my children grew up and I got older, I looked for additional challenges beyond just work. In 1999, I began to train and run again, something I hadn't done in a very long time. Mostly because of a dare and a long-standing desire to lose some weight, I started to think about running a longer race and over the next two years, ran in more than 20 events longer than 13.1 miles, the official distance for a half marathon. I was never a competitive runner by any means, but enjoyed the training aspect and the focus it provided on reaching a specific goal. During my training, we took a family vacation to England to visit relatives and sightsee, and I ran every day through the streets of London and Gloucester, often at my own peril, as my sense of traffic was still based on the right side of the street drivers in the U.S.

In October of 2000, I successfully completed my first marathon, running the 26.2 miles of the Milwaukee Lakefront Marathon in just over 4 hours and 45 minutes. One of my greatest memories is crossing the finish line of that race, completing the journey that I had begun over a year earlier.

In 2006, I met Richard Bolender, the mayor of Oak Creek at the time, at a community event. We had talked briefly about what was going on in the city and Mayor Bolender asked me if I had any interest in serving on a standing committee or board. These were volunteer positions, but provided input to the elected officials on issues related to many of the city's core functions. He appointed me to the zoning board, and at the same time, I attempted a run for Mayor in 2006. Although I felt I was known well enough by the community to make a successful run for mayor, I finished a dismal third in the primaries. It was the first of two straight election losses — I would also run unsuccessfully for aldermen in 2007 — losing by just 15 votes.

Since that time, I've won every race I've entered, serving two terms as alderman before winning the 2012 election for mayor. I actually served as an interim mayor for a couple weeks in 2011 after Mayor Bolender died unexpectedly in office, while I was Common Council President. It certainly gave me a heads up on what the position was about, and probably gave some residents the confidence that I could serve in that position when I came up for election in April of 2012.

One of the most common questions I'm asked is why I ran for office in the first place. Seeking public office certainly isn't for financial gain, as my current salary as mayor is $16,000. But as someone who appreciates what public service can do when it functions properly, I've always been frustrated by the lack of vision and integrity of elected officials who spend more of their time on the politics of getting elected than the hard work of actually getting things done. Perhaps it was my background in the private sector, or just the values instilled in me by my parents, but accomplishments have always been more important to me than being elected. Whatever credit I get as a result of our work on the response and recovery from the Sikh Temple shooting is a byproduct of that public service mission. I've met many people in public service who also exemplify that, including Steve Hogan from Aurora, Colorado, whose wisdom and guidance helped me get through the difficult first few days after August 5, 2012.

Just one week before I was elected as Mayor of the City of Oak Creek in April of 2012, I spent my last day working for the Nielsen Company. I didn't know it then of course, but in four months, I would be tested in ways I had never thought of, and would literally spend the next year dealing almost exclusively with our community's response to the events at the Sikh Temple of Wisconsin. For me, my new role was about learning as much as I could in a very short amount of time, but one that my experiences and background had certainly prepared me for.

An Uncommon Bond between Mayors

The winter meeting of the U.S. Conference of Mayors is held every January in Washington, D.C. In 2013, I attended my first meeting as mayor and along with hundreds of other mayors from across the country heard presentations on the economy, education, and other challenges facing each of our communities and the country. Philadelphia Mayor Michael Nutter was the chairman of the Conference of Mayors, and I had met him just a day earlier when he sat next to me at the White House for the President's speech on gun violence.

Once settled in to the conference, I met many of the other mayors from cities small and large as we moved from room to room at the Capitol Hilton and heard presentations from Cabinet Secretaries and heads of other government agencies. Vice-President Joe Biden spoke to the assembled crowd at lunch during the conference, and I noticed the ramped-up security at the entrances and exits of the building, the threat of violence never too far away.

Joining me from Wisconsin was Mayor Steven Ponto from Brookfield, a city located just west of Milwaukee in Waukesha County. Mayor Ponto had just endured a mass shooting in his own community in October, just two months after the shooting at the Sikh Temple. The gunman had killed three people, including his own wife, at a spa in

152

Brookfield before turning the gun on himself. In a clear case of domestic violence, the shooter had purchased a gun in a quick cash transaction to avoid a background check, and despite a restraining order against him, took a cab to his wife's place of work. Once inside, he killed her and two of her co-workers. Mayor Ponto and I had communicated briefly before the conference as he was selected as my mentor since I was a first-time attendee. We sat together at a few of the presentations during the conference but we had arranged to meet with three other mayors for lunch on Friday, the last day of the conference. Unfortunately, all of us shared an uncommon bond. Each of us were the mayors of cities that had been the scene of a mass shooting.

We met inside the cafe at the Capitol Hilton just down the main staircase from the conference rooms. Some of us had already met at the conference; some were meeting each other for the first time. There were five of us at the table including myself; Mayor Ponto, Mayor Ron Rordam of Blacksburg, Virginia, Steven Hogan from Aurora, Colorado, and Mayor Jonathan Rothschild from Tucson, Arizona.

The leaders at the table had all experienced the worst examples of how violence can impact a community. Blacksburg, Virginia was the home of Virginia Tech University and the scene of the deadliest mass shooting in U.S. History. On April 16, 2007, a 23-year-old student killed

32 people and himself in and around the Virginia Tech campus. Just three weeks prior to the 2012 Sikh Temple shooting, a shooter dressed in military-style clothing opened fire in a movie theater in Aurora, Colorado. He eventually killed 12 people and wounded 70 more. In January of 2011, at a constituent event for Congresswoman Gabby Giffords in the Tucson area, a gunman opened fire and killed six people, including a nine-year-old girl, and wounding the Congresswoman.

All of us had direct experiences related to gun violence in our communities. Each had gone through the aftermath of a mass shooting and the stages of shock, grief, and recovery that followed it. As we went around the table, we talked about our events and how we dealt with them, both from a leadership perspective and personally. I learned details about each of the events beyond just a grim recounting of the number of lives lost. For each of the leaders, there was profound respect for what the other mayors had endured.

Mayor Hogan called me in the evening after the shooting at our Sikh Temple and offered me his guidance based on what he had just gone through in his city. I have reached out several times to local leaders who have experienced a mass shooting to extend my thoughts and prayers to their communities. It's not an empty gesture and certainly not one expecting a response, but in some way, the act of reaching out can link leaders together and hopefully, whenever help is needed, a direct contact point is ready. In an interview I did with a national newspaper during the first week after the Temple shooting, I talked about the role of leadership beyond the borders of a city, and what I could do to share any wisdom I've gained during my experience. Mayor Hogan's insights certainly helped me.

Mayor Rordam and I sat together during the conference and shared many aspects of our lives and how the shooting impacted us. We both had been invited to the White House for the President's speech and were mentioned by name in Mayor Michael Bloomberg's speech to the conference on gun violence. We were also wary of being labeled as "anti-gun" since we both believed that gun rights were important and that the real issues were more complex than that. Talking about gun violence was often enough to worry constituents, especially if you lived in a conservative part of the country. That's a sad commentary on the debate, and probably one of the biggest reasons why little has been done to address gun violence in any meaningful way.

The bond between the five mayors was significant. It was a small club, one that you really don't want to be a part of. Knowing that these other leaders had gone through it, and had experienced what I had just gone through, it was therapeutic. As we wrapped up, we exchanged our contact information and took a group picture in the lobby of the hotel. All of us had shared experiences with violence in settings as diverse as a theater, campus, supermarket parking lot, and a Temple. We had all seen unspeakable horror and violence yet carried on in our roles, hopeful that something could be done to change it in the future.

John's Shooting

Throughout the days and months after the Sikh Temple shooting Police Chief John Edwards had to call upon his 25 years of experience in law enforcement to lead the department through this difficult period, including nearly losing an officer. Although he had been in the leadership position for just over a year, John had served in nearly every capacity in the department during his long career, including 13 years as a member of the SWAT Emergency Response Unit, which deals with high-risk, potentially lethal hostage and gun violence situations.

When we went to Froedtert Hospital on the evening of August 5, meeting with Murphy's family and the police officers standing watch just outside his room, it was easy to see in his conversations, and in the guidance and support he showed for his fellow officers, that John was calling upon his first-hand knowledge of officer-involved shootings. Most of the world wasn't aware of it, but he had been there before. Twenty-three years earlier, he had come face to face with his own mortality in a truck stop parking lot in Oak Creek.

Just after 4:00 a.m. on the morning of March 25, 1989, during an early morning parking lot sweep of license plates, a practice that law enforcement still uses today to identify vehicles whose drivers may have outstanding

157

warrants, John came upon a suspicious-looking vehicle. He didn't know it when he stopped, but the vehicle was driven by an escaped prisoner from a federal prison in Indiana, who had no intention of returning to incarceration. As he approached the car, the escapee, Ronald R. Plummer, got out of his vehicle with a gun in each hand, and ordered John to get on the ground. Recalling the incident years later, John said that because he wasn't expecting the escapee to come out with guns drawn, he didn't have his gun out. He had only two options: get down on the ground, or run. John's instinct and training told him to ignore that command. He turned sideways and began to run. Plummer fired, hitting John in the badge, a fortunate circumstance that may have saved his life. Plummer, and an accomplice, Elizabeth Bonvillian, who aided in his escape, fled the scene. They were both eventually captured after ending up in a deserted barn just south of Oak Creek.

John's original badge now framed and hanging on the wall in the Oak Creek Police Department was ripped from his shirt, taking the brunt of the impact. It had prevented the bullet from entering his chest. A second shot hit him in the right index finger. This incident was one of the first officer-involved shootings in Oak Creek and gave John a harsh introduction to the risks faced every day in the life of a police officer. After treatment and release from the hospital, John spent three months in recovery before returning to active duty, struggling with the after-effects of the shooting, admitting years later that he probably had post-traumatic-stress-disorder for some time after the shooting, perhaps as long as two years. John also told me that looking back at that time, the department had a "suck it up" mentality, making it difficult for any officer to seek help for issues related to stress, even in the case of police shootings. He admitted he struggled with the decision to remain a police officer, perhaps feeling his own mortality so early on in his career.

Having known John for more than 35 years, it was easy from a communications perspective to be on the same page. After all, we not only worked together but also spent a lot of time away from the job on golf courses, deer hunting trips, and in our younger days, playing on the same softball and basketball teams. Considering his background, and his depth of experience as a police officer, Oak Creek was in good hands in the hours and days after the shooting. His coolness under fire and his ability to delegate almost immediately were key aspects of the response and the investigation into the shooting.

The crime scene was handed over to the FBI almost immediately after the shooting, but Oak Creek's Police Department was handling the investigation of the work of Murphy and Lenda, their responses to the scene, and their interactions with the shooter Wade Michael Page. Given the scale of this investigation, it made sense to hand significant parts of the work over to the FBI, who had already committed a large number of personnel and assets to the crime scene. Milwaukee's Special Agent in Charge Teresa Carlson had participated in the August 6 press conference and had also been present for the almost daily meetings during the first week with the Temple representatives, local agencies, and the Department of Justice. She was the second woman ever to lead the Milwaukee office of the FBI. She had a tough no-nonsense approach to the investigation, voicing her opinion right away that the FBI had to take over the bulk of the investigation due to the scope of the shooting, and its ties to white supremacist groups.

During the weeks and months after the shooting, there would be tension between Chief Edwards and Special Agent Carlson. Both had very strong personalities, and the perceived slowness of the clearing of information related to the conduct of our officers, particularly Lenda, who was patiently waiting to get back to active duty, caused some ripples within Oak Creek's police department. At a closed door meeting a week after the shooting, Agent Carlson had also made some perceived derogatory comments in the absence of Chief Edwards — who was on a previously scheduled vacation — and had angered both of the Captains on the department, straining the relationship even further. Agent Carlson felt strongly that the schedule of events related to the release of our dash-cam video, which showed the tremendous police work done by all of our first-responders, specifically Murphy and Lenda, would be released on the FBI's schedule, despite the fact that the video was the property of Oak Creek. In the opinion of the City Attorney Larry Haskin, it would demonstrate the great police work done by both officers. I enthusiastically agreed, and from the city perspective, it certainly would show the public, second by second, the incredible police work that was done on August 5, 2012.

Regardless of the conflicts or disagreements between the FBI and the Oak Creek Police Department, the conduct of the officers was reviewed independently by Milwaukee County District Attorney John Chisholm, a prosecutor who had established a strong reputation for careful and thorough review of all officer-involved shootings. Chisholm's report cleared the officers, and put Lenda back on the street, something he had been itching to do since the day after the shooting.

Almost immediately after the shooting, John was bombarded with requests to speak at seminars and conferences on Oak Creek's response to the mass shooting incident. Unlike many law enforcement leaders, John was not hesitant to talk about great police work, and in his mind, the importance of training and development, critical pieces of the department's commitment to community

safety. John credited the department's previous
leadership, specifically former Police Chief Thomas Bauer,
who led the department for the fourteen years before
Chief Edwards had taken command, and had advocated
for most of the initiatives that defined the department's
philosophy of community-based policing. John and
Murphy appeared together at a Police Officer of the Year
conference in San Diego, California in October of 2012,
Murphy still healing from his multiple wounds.

The Oak Creek Police Department viewed the relationship
between the community and the department as critical to
achieving results in crime response and prevention. The
department had a strong *Crime Stoppers* program, and a
full-time Community Resource officer, Kim Bogadi,
devoted to outreach and improved communication, two
critical pieces in building a safer community. As John
developed a presentation related to the events of August
5, which he used around the country at various speaking
appearances, he also gradually pieced together a template
of guiding principles for engagement and community
relations. Many were groundbreaking in their scope and
raised the profile of the department beyond what it had
already achieved with its response to the Temple shooting.
He spelled them out in an article in *Police Chief Magazine*
that he co-authored with Libby McInerny, Director of
Strategic Partnerships and Campaign Development for *Not
in Our Town*, an Oakland-based nonprofit which highlights

communities that work together to stop hate.

The guidelines highlight the perceived strengths of the department, including continuing education and training for police officers, officer wellness programs, proactive policing with clear transparency, and strong engagement with the public. These practices ensure that a trust is established, making residents comfortable enough to report crimes when they see them. But the critical piece of the puzzle for local law enforcement, at least in the minds of our police department and city leadership, is strong media engagement. This not only builds a perception that the community is open and honest in their dealings with the public but also aids in the dissemination of information when necessary, reducing the spread of rumors or misinformation, which can impact police investigations. This direct link can build trust, a key component of establishing direct links to the community that you serve.

John and I had learned a lot about the role of the media in the aftermath of the Temple shooting. From our initial early morning efforts on Monday, August 6, our communication skills and comfort level in front of the cameras had certainly improved, but the realization that they could be also be a partner was now a key element of the story. Film and video projects related to the Temple shooting were beginning to show up. They would tell the story in a different way. One with a much deeper and

thought-provoking view of the significance of the Oak
Creek tragedy, told from the point of view of not only the
Sikh community, but also through the eyes of people
committed to changing the focus from the act of violence,
to ways to stop it from happening at all.

Telling Our Story

As soon as the next day after the shooting, nationally known filmmakers were on the ground in Oak Creek, beginning to tell the story of the Sikh Temple shooting, the impact on the victims' families, and our community's reactions. As Chief Edwards and I moved from interview to interview at the Police Department, City Hall, and the growing makeshift media village just across the street from the Temple, we also took the time to sit down with two groups of filmmakers who would eventually document the aftermath of August 5, 2012 from a national perspective.

Valarie Kaur and her husband Sharat Raju arrived in Oak Creek on Tuesday, August 7 and spent weeks interviewing and filming at the Temple, City Hall, the Police Station, and around the city, capturing the images and voices of Oak Creek. Valarie is the founder of *Groundswell Movement*, the nation's largest multi-faith online organizing community, based at Auburn Seminary. She delivered thousands of prayers and letters of support that Groundswell had collected for the Oak Creek community.

Growing up in Central California, the descendent of *Punjabi* Sikh farmers, Valarie is a national interfaith leader who has fought for civil rights through her films and advocacy campaigns. She has led awareness for Sikh rights

165

as well as documented the racism and harassment of Muslims and Sikhs after 9/11. Sharat is a writer and director known for his critically-acclaimed short film *American Made* about a Sikh American family and their struggle to fit into American society. Together they made *Divided We Fall,* considered the definitive documentary on hate crimes in the aftermath of 9/11.

As a Sikh activist who had documented hate crimes against her community, Valarie not only understood the pain of our Temple community from a personal perspective, but also the broader stakes for a country struggling with race, religion, and violence. Her incredible storytelling and ability to link the individual with the culture made her an authority on Sikh faith and history in America, leading to appearances on national news programs in the days after the shooting. She was one of many young Sikh Americans, both in the Midwest and nationally, who worked tirelessly to help our community grieve and tell our story to the world.

Valarie and Sharat's project, *Oak Creek: In Memoriam* examined the shooting and the 45 days after, capturing in nine minutes the terror felt by the men, women, and children of the Temple on the morning of August 5 and how Oak Creek responded to the shooting.

Watching their film, both in a public setting and in private,

I'm taken back to the first moments of the shooting and the days after. Much of my short tenure as mayor was also tied in with the shooting, and in the events related to it. In those first few weeks, I attended FBI briefings, meetings with the Temple families, vigils, funeral services, prayer meetings, and press conferences. Each of these public and private events was focused on the tragedy and how we might deal with that going forward.

As I hear the voices of the Temple families, the great sense of loss they feel, and their struggle in those first few days to deal with this new reality, it's difficult not to share that grief. I've come to know them, not just because they worship in Oak Creek, but because I've been linked to them by a shared sense of disbelief and pain that comes with the knowledge that it happened here and to people that I now know personally.

In January of 2013 we screened *Oak Creek: In Memoriam* at an anti-violence summit at one of our Oak Creek schools. In fact, we led the discussion by first viewing the film, and then introducing some of the individuals in it to the hundreds of people in attendance. Pardeep Kaleka, Chief John Edwards, U.S. Attorney James Santelle, Milwaukee County Executive Chris Abele and I were part of a panel discussion, moderated by local television anchor and reporter Annie Scholz of NBC affiliate WTMJ, along with other experts in mental health, interfaith relations,

167

public safety, and community violence.

This summit honored a commitment that both the Chief and I had made to the families that we would not let the horrific events of August 5 fade from the public's attention. We both recognized early on that the significance of that day went beyond our borders. It touched a national and international audience who not only felt connected by faith, in the case of the millions of Sikhs worldwide, but also in a shared sentiment that the mass shootings in the U.S. in the last half of 2012 had brought out widespread concerns about access to guns, cultural acceptance and diversity, and mental health. I shared that belief. The summit was a first step in reaching out beyond Oak Creek to talk about some of these issues.

At the same time Valarie and Sharat had been working on their film, an Oakland, California-based production company had also expressed an interest in interviewing the Chief and me about our experiences related to the shootings. *Not in our Town*, a nationally acclaimed public television series of films about local community movements to stop hate and violence, along with their parent company *The Working Group* had contacted our offices about sending a film crew on the Friday of the funeral services in Oak Creek. Inspired by the actions of the residents of Billings, Montana in 1995, *Not in our Town* tells the story of communities in the U.S. that stand up against hatred and violence. From their perspective, Oak Creek had already taken the first key steps into making that a reality.

Immediately after the funeral services, Chief Edwards and I sat down with a film crew based out of Chicago and Milwaukee and reviewed the details of the case from a law enforcement and local government perspective. They were long interviews, stretching out over several hours, in much greater depth than most of the media interviews we had done during the week. We were asked about how the shootings had affected our community, how we responded, and where we would go from here.

Only five days had passed since the shooting, my emotions were still very raw, and much of what I felt about August 5 and its broader impact was still forming in my brain. But the belief that our response could define this story, and how we went forward as a city that had witnessed a brutal act of violence, drove me to a deeper, more thoughtful consideration of the shootings, and gave me a willingness to participate in the national discussion.

Producer and filmmaker Patrice O'Neill and her crew traveled to Oak Creek many times during 2013, capturing interviews and images from many of the community events linked to the shooting, including the one year anniversary of the shooting. The memorial honoring the victims took place on the land immediately adjacent to the Sikh Temple on a cloudy Monday evening in August. The candlelight vigil connected Oak Creek to the more recent tragedy in Newtown, Connecticut, with testimonials from family members, faith groups, and civil rights leaders from around the country.

More than a thousand people showed up to honor the victims, and the significance of that event was not lost on the NIOT producers, who had multiple cameras on the grounds as it unfolded. Moderated by Amardeep Kaleka and Valarie Kaur, the evening was both sad and festive, symbolizing the horror of that day in August 2012 but also highlighting the many emerging and positive initiatives that had grown out of it.

We premiered *Waking in Oak Creek* at the Oak Creek Community Center on March 13, 2014. In front of more than 500 residents, community leaders, and many of the family members from our local Sikh Temple, the film brought back many of the images and scenes I had remembered from the shooting and its aftermath. Seated in many rows across the full length of the center's main room with three large screens showing the film, the audience cried and even laughed at one point as Murphy talked about his injuries and how they had canceled a planned vacation with his wife Ann. As the film moved from the shooting, to the community response and

Murphy's amazing recovery, it reminded me of the journey that we had been on in the days since August 2012. The film ends with the inaugural *Chardi Kala* 6K event, which I ran in, held at our local high school to honor the victims and to commemorate the one-year anniversary of the shooting. As the credits rolled, I looked over a crowd of people who understood that a horrible thing had happened here, but despite that tragedy the community had come together, exactly the opposite reaction Wade Michael Page had intended.

Each of the Sikh Temple-related events that happened in the year after the shooting played a role in our city's recovery, and in our ability to not only cope with what happened, but in telling the story of why Oak Creek could offer a response that didn't accept hatred or violence against people who were perceived as different.

Guns were a part of our story, despite the uncomfortable nature of that topic to some. We had moved from shock to grief to healing, and now we were starting to talk about how gun violence influences our society and daily lives. Too soon, it was clear that the framing of that issue would fall back into well-worn, entrenched arguments that drew a line in the sand between gun rights and the public's right to safety and security in their neighborhoods, their homes, and in their places of worship.

Son of the Temple President

Amardeep Kaleka is the youngest son of Satwant Singh Kaleka, the president and founder of the Sikh Temple of Wisconsin who was brutally killed in the attack on August 5, 2012. In the days following the shooting, Amardeep, an Emmy-award winning filmmaker who at the time of the shooting lived in southern California, quickly became the public face of the Sikh community. His appearances on CNN's *Anderson Cooper 360* and MSNBC, also speaking eloquently at both the vigil and the funeral services, connected the Sikh immigrant story with the broader American public. His easy style and soothing tone made him a natural for the media and he went on network and local television to tell the story of the Sikhs and the impact of the tragedy on his family and their community.

His message was not necessarily the same as the Temple leadership, and he was quick to point out that he represented the families and not the Temple, a distinction that would be apparent at several events in the months after the shooting. Amardeep was vocal, unusual in a group who typically did not seek out public attention, regardless of circumstance. He was savvy enough to understand that a platform was opening in front of him and he was not afraid to take a stand on it or other difficult issues including civil rights, gun control, or politics. In the months following the shooting, he created the video

172

We are Sikhs and created a donation platform to raise money for the victim's families.

I first met Amardeep on the Tuesday of the vigil and it was easy to see both his ease with the media and his willingness to speak his mind. He'd done that often in the months and year since the shooting. Soon after the shooting, he challenged President Obama to visit Oak Creek, something the President had done after the Aurora shooting, to meet with the families and to raise the national awareness of the Sikh community. A story of immigrants and America that Amardeep wanted to so desperately to tell. The President sent First Lady Michelle Obama instead, who eventually met with the families, the Temple leadership, and myself two weeks after the shooting. For some in the Sikh community this was considered to be snub, since the President had just recently flown to Colorado to meet with the theater victim's families after the Aurora shooting. To her credit the First Lady spent a significant amount of a day in the community, but the fact that the President of the United States didn't visit the scene of one of the worst acts of violence in our nation's history, committed in a place of worship, certainly raised some eyebrows.

I've had the chance to talk with Amardeep many times since then, and his spirit and his willingness to engage in broader discussions is immediately evident in every conversation. Nourished by his passion for change and his concern that violence was consuming the collective consciousness of our country and in his mind probably contributed to the killing of his father, he looked to a national platform beyond interviews and talk shows. Late in 2013, he made the decision to run for the 1st Congressional District seat currently held by Congressman Paul Ryan, a very popular elected official in Wisconsin whose district contained Oak Creek and much of southeastern Wisconsin. A rising star in the Republican Party and a six-term congressman, Ryan was Mitt Romney's choice for Vice President in his 2012 unsuccessful campaign for President. Despite that loss, Paul Ryan maintained his considerable popularity both in Wisconsin and nationally, and for Amardeep it meant fighting an uphill battle against a candidate who routinely wins by double-digit margins. Kaleka would lose to Ron Zerban in the Democratic primary.

At the time of the shooting Amardeep was driving to the Temple with his wife and his two-year-old son. He began to hear the reports on the radio of a shooting in Oak Creek, and his older brother Pardeep called him and said there had been a shooting at the Temple. As he drove, Amardeep received a call from his father's cell phone, and he answered it. On the phone was Bhai Sahib Gurmail Singh, a priest at the Temple, who told him that his father had been shot in the back and was bleeding profusely.

Amardeep asked to speak with him, but Singh told him
that his father could no longer speak.

He quickly called his mother Satpal who had hidden in the
pantry in the kitchen to escape Page's rampage. Her voice
whispering "I don't know if he's still inside" to his frantic
questions to her about the gunman and his father's
condition. He made his way to Oak Creek before being
stopped at the intersection of Rawson and Howell
avenues, just north of the Temple. At a Cousin's Sub shop
just west of the intersection, Amardeep met his brother
Pardeep and his cousin Kanwardeep Singh Kaleka, each
desperately trying to find a path around the police
barricades to get to their father's side inside the Temple.

After a few aborted attempts to reach the Temple, the
Kalekas gave up and were directed by police officers to
Classic Lanes. It was just across the street from the Temple
and served as a gathering place and care center for the
families. They would wait there until much later in the day,
finally finding out around 10:00 p.m. that their father was
one of the victims. There was a brief moment of awkward
confusion in the notification process as an Oak Creek
police detective mixed up the names of *Santokh Singh*,
who was wounded in the attack and treated at a local
hospital, and their father, *Satwant Singh*, before the
mistake was finally realized and corrected. For Amardeep,
it was just a final confirmation of what he had feared all

day since receiving the first few calls.

The exact details of what happened inside the Temple on August 5, 2012, are difficult to know for certain given how quickly the shootings happened, the absence of video surveillance, and the chaos created inside the Temple. But what is clear from both eyewitness accounts and the details inside the FBI report on the shooting is that Amardeep's father, Satwant Singh Kaleka, 65 years old at the time of his death, fought with Wade Michael Page near the end of his rampage and died in his efforts to stop him. According to Amardeep, his elderly father struggled valiantly with the younger Page, defending the Temple that he built. He tried to stop Page from shooting anyone else in the Temple before being shot to death himself. It's easy to hear his love for his father as he talks about him and also his frustration with the lack of progress in the national conversation about violence in this country, calling America's obsession with guns and violence a "cultural habit bordering on obsession."

Amardeep came to the United States in 1982 at the age of three, his father moving his young family from political upheaval in India to the inner city of Milwaukee. His father worked in gas stations as a clerk, exposing his young sons to a tough environment in a primarily poor, black neighborhood. His upbringing and his experiences as a young Sikh growing up in the United States provided a backdrop for his future career as a filmmaker. He used those skills to tell the story of violence in America in a feature documentary film called *Peacemakers*, which Amardeep and his company Neverending Light Productions will release in 2015. The film project, begun in April of 2012, looked for answers to the issues of violence in our country, and ironically explored the recent rise in acts of violence in America prior to the shooting in Oak Creek. The killing of his father tragically provided an immediate and shocking example for Amardeep, who was now front and center in a national debate on violence and responsible gun ownership, and he began the trailer of the film with the last words of his father as he talked to the 911 dispatchers at the Oak Creek Police Department.

The shooting at the Oak Creek *gurdwara* closely followed the Aurora, Colorado theater shooting and preceded, only by a few months, the massacre of 26 young children, their teachers, and administrators at Sandy Hook Elementary in Newtown, Connecticut. With Oak Creek's place in the national consciousness now firmly set, Amardeep's direction was also laid out in front of him. He would honor his father and the other victims with a commitment to involving the greater community in a call to action, creating the beginnings of a social movement aimed at stopping what was becoming a rapidly rising tide of violence in America. In the Milwaukee area, Amardeep and his brother Pardeep launched the youth organization

Serve2Unite to mentor students to build nonviolent and compassionate environments in their schools and communities.

As I began to learn the story of our local Sikh Temple and understand the tragedy from a personal perspective, it was clear that many in our community also saw a flicker of hope for a national discussion on issues ranging from an awareness of the Sikh faith to recognition of Sikhs in FBI statistics on hate crimes, to the acceptance of Sikh customs in the military. All of these concerns were amplified after August 5, 2012, and to their credit, the members of the Temple carried on the legacy of their lost family members by speaking out and organizing whenever they could on these issues. A broader national discussion was also unfolding in neighborhoods, newsrooms, and in the minds of elected officials across the country. That conversation would also gain the attention of the most influential political leader in the world, and create a firestorm of debate on the role of guns and the 2nd Amendment in our society.

The Gun Debate

Whenever you bring up the subject of gun violence in our country, the level of discourse generally degrades fairly quickly to a 2nd Amendment versus gun control argument. Good people, with significant education and real life experiences dealing with the impact of guns in cities across America will often abandon reasoned argument for an all-or-nothing defense of gun rights or a simplistic ban-all-guns argument, which essentially takes the U.S. Constitution and throws it out the window.

Given what happened in Oak Creek, it's understandable that the debate would come to my city, and I would be asked by residents, media, gun rights groups and other organizations about my stance on guns and their place in our society. We had six people killed in their place of worship on a beautiful Sunday morning, and the significance of that event still weighed heavily on Oak Creek, and specifically the families at the Temple, who were still grieving. The details of the shooting, the fact that the guns used were obtained legally, didn't matter to the spouses, sons and daughters, and other relatives of the victims whose lives would be changed forever because of this act of hate.

As a teenager growing up in Wisconsin, I had hunted with my father many times. I can remember jumping up and

down on a wood pile at the edge of a farm field as my dad
waited for rabbits to dart out from their cover, the sound
of the shotgun blast startling me. I had grown up with
hunting and the annual deer hunt, not unusual in a state
like Wisconsin. Growing up around guns, taking hunter-
safety courses before being handed a shotgun, was part of
the experience. I understood that guns should be taken
seriously, given their power and their ability to take a life.

Fairly soon after the Temple shooting, I was asked about
my feelings on guns and whether or not their use should
be restricted or more tightly regulated. I feel strongly that
gun ownership is a right guaranteed by the Constitution,
but that much more needed to be done to make sure that
guns stayed out of the hands of people who shouldn't
have them, whether that was because of a criminal record,
certain mental health concerns, or other behavioral issues.
The recent shooting in Aurora, Colorado had
demonstrated the danger of guns in the hands of
individuals incapable or unwilling to use them responsibly
— 12 people killed in the act of watching a movie,
ironically the Batman movie *The Dark Knight Rises.*

The school shooting in December of 2012 in Newtown,
Connecticut put an exclamation point on the argument
that we needed to take a harder look at how guns are
distributed in our society. We needed to examine how
much we are willing to tolerate the risk of violence,

balanced against the right of every American to own a gun. As much as groups like the National Rifle Association would like to think that guns and their use need no restrictions, clearly that's not the case. I don't think most people have an issue with the restrictions on guns on airplanes or in courtrooms, and it's clear that U.S. courts understand that limits can and should be in place to ensure public safety. Finding the proper balance between a citizen's constitutional rights and the public's expectation for reasonable public safety and security is not easy — it never has been in our country's history. But if the cycle of mass shootings in 2012 says anything, we need to take a closer look.

As early as the week after the Oak Creek shooting, gun control was on most people's mind. The nightly cable news programs talked about it, Reverend Jesse Jackson had talked about it in his remarks at the services for the victims, and several members of the victims' families had mentioned it to me in conversations that week. But much of what passes for public discussion on the issue is usually post-event, triggered by a "what can I do?" gut response which probably has its roots in psychology, or a natural instinct to want to help someone who has suffered. All of us feel and react strongly when we see lives ended prematurely, violently, especially when that act happens in a setting where you wouldn't expect it.

Reasonable, rational people can disagree on the subject of guns, and how much control or regulation is appropriate or constitutionally acceptable. Irrational people, in my opinion, don't see the distinction, and often look for opportunity in tragedy, or evidence to support their belief that any infringement — *there's that sticky word of Constitutional ambiguity* — is an assault on personal freedom. But where is the role of social responsibility? What responsibility do we have for the victims and their families to make sure that their lives were not lost in vain? As a democratic country founded on rights and principles, shouldn't we look for every opportunity to improve our society in the hard lessons of our history?

As I talked with the media after August 5, I was often asked the question of how guns fit into the story and whether we should have stricter gun control in the U.S. From that week on, I've slowly realized that we should frame the argument in terms of gun violence, not gun control. Say the words "gun control", and the argument deteriorates quickly. Talk about gun violence and prevention, and you at least have the opportunity to have a conversation.

So much of the story of Oak Creek, Aurora, Newtown and other cities where mass shootings have occurred involve individuals who have demonstrated an inability to make rational decisions in their own lives and have chosen violence as a means of acting out, or taking out their anger and hatred on others. Guns have served as the method of delivery, but as we saw in Oak Creek, Aurora, and Newton if a gun is purchased legally, how do we reduce the likelihood that a person uses it to take a life? Clearly in our case, the shooter, Wade Michael Page, had a problem with alcohol abuse and developmental issues going back into his childhood. His willingness to embrace the extremist ideologies of the Hammerskins white supremacist group gave him an outlet for his anger, but it isn't clear where the final push to take violent action against the Sikh community came from.

Page lived in a nearby city, six miles away from the Temple, and it's uncertain whether he ever came into contact with members of the Temple at some point in the past, or simply stumbled upon the Temple one day while driving around the area. What is clear is that between his residence in the City of Cudahy and the Howell Avenue location of the Sikh Temple of Wisconsin, there are numerous places of worship that had members who looked more like Page. When Page took his own life in the parking lot at the Sikh Temple of Wisconsin, whatever motive he had died with him. The FBI and other agencies tasked with investigating Page found little evidence beyond his affiliations with the Hammerskins to establish a motive for the killings. In my mind, there is little doubt that this was a hate crime.

So absent a clear motive, what does the Oak Creek shooting tell us about guns, violence, or even the lack of cultural acceptance and diversity in our country? Throwing up your hands, or employing the famous bumper sticker slogan *guns don't kill people, people kill people* isn't particularly illuminating logic, given that both an individual and a gun are necessary partners in the committing of the act of shooting someone. Page purchased his weapons legally, found the time to visit a local shooting range to target shoot, and despite his rather violent, hate-filled background in the years leading up to 2012, his criminal record was fairly light. Without a direct link to violence in his background, it's highly unlikely that people like Page could be stopped *before* they commit heinous acts like the Sikh Temple shooting.

Aurora and Newtown are somewhat different stories. Their shooters also used legally obtained guns to commit their acts, but both James Holmes and Adam Lanza, the shooters in Aurora and Newton, clearly had serious, documented mental health issues leading up to their acts of violence. In both cases, and at critical points in their lives, failures in family, their respective communities, and perhaps our society in general, contributed to their ultimate acts of hate. Both men demonstrated through their actions, their private conversations with mental health professionals and in their behavior immediately before their shootings, that they had taken a mental step forward in making the decision to act out. In Holmes' case, he had purchased weapons and large amounts of ammunition in the months prior to the theater shooting. Adam Lanza's mother, Nancy Lanza, who was described by her sister as a "gun enthusiast," a somewhat curious hobby given her son's personal story, owned many weapons, including the guns used by Adam Lanza at Sandy Hook elementary school. She encouraged her son to go with her to a local gun range, despite the indications that her son had a fascination with violence.

What these three cases suggest is that despite the current state of gun legislation in America, including background checks, each of these mass shootings probably would have happened regardless of what measures would have been put in place to stop them. But what they do show is that there is a significant disconnect between the mental health community, and at least the perception of a hesitancy or unwillingness of families and their medical professionals to intervene before events like this occur. Walking the line between mental health and gun rights is a particularly tricky subject, given individual's right to medical records privacy, and in medical professionals' reluctance to step over that line. However, the question remains, does the public good carry extra weight given what could happen, and what did take place in 2012? Much of what should be the focus of legislation going forward needs to understand that the prevention of violence goes much deeper than guns.

Given that guns are the principal means of violence in our country, we must examine what we can do as a society to limit the public's risk of being killed by a weapon that was illegally obtained. Gun background checks do work, and many individuals who shouldn't own guns have been prevented from buying them, perhaps saving many lives in the process. Overwhelmingly, Americans support enforceable and easy-to-administer background checks. This has been widely reported, and even the vast majority of the NRA's members agree.

When I was asked by the *Mayors Against Illegal Guns* organization to support their efforts to encourage the President and Congress to support common sense gun legislation, I made it clear that what I support is a background check policy that works as close to 100% of the time as possible. Enforcement of background checks and ensuring public safety by keeping guns out of the hands of people who shouldn't own them must be the priority.

Joining any lobbying group, particularly one associated with gun rights or proposed gun legislation, will always be controversial, even for a mayor of a city who has suffered through a mass shooting. In my case, my participation was viewed by many as a willingness to abandon the 2nd

Amendment and to trample on the rights of individuals to own guns. As I've said, I own guns, and use them throughout the year to hunt. I believe strongly that every American is born with the right, if they wish, to own a gun, and understand that the Constitution implicitly says that. What it doesn't say is that individuals who our society says are no longer entitled to those rights, like felons, should be able to circumvent the system, and purchase weapons illegally, or without a proper background check being performed. Saying that the background check process is broken doesn't mean that we shouldn't attempt to fix it, or to put even more stringent measures in place to guarantee, as best we can, that those persons buying weapons are entitled to do so.

As my participation and membership in the *Mayors Against Illegal Guns* group became public, particularly after attending the President's press conference on proposed gun legislation at the White House, I began to receive emails and letters expressing displeasure with my willingness to join an organization sponsored by then New York Mayor Michael Bloomberg. Several people purposely changed the name to *Mayors Against Guns* in a rather disingenuous attempt to classify me as anti-gun, not bothering to listen to what I actually said on the subject. Some email writers threatened me; some said they would work to throw me out of office unless I withdrew my support for MAIG. What I continue to say on the issue is that all Americans should be in favor of strict, properly administered background checks, regardless of their position on the 2nd Amendment. We correctly enforce legal, responsible limits to all aspects of our life every day, owning guns should be treated no differently, with respect to the intent and integrity of the Constitution.

I'll continue to speak out on the issue, and to reinforce what I think is a realistic, intellectually honest approach to gun rights, understanding that the complexity of the debate in our country requires a thoughtful and reasoned examination of the link between guns, how they are purchased, and who should ultimately have access to them.

Gurpreet

When I sat down to talk with Gurpreet Dulai almost 20 months after the Temple shooting, at a Starbucks just a mile away from the Sikh Temple, I was immediately struck by her confidence. A college student studying pharmacy and a Sikh who has lived her entire life in the United States, she demonstrated a sense of commitment to her faith, balanced with a sometimes pessimistic view of what the future holds for the country and the world. She had represented the youth of the Temple at the vigil held on August 7, and looking back at her words that night, her voice shaking as she addressed the large crowd, she was clearly still in shock from what she had witnessed just two days earlier. She was one of the first family members on the scene, arriving almost simultaneously as the first-responding officers, prompted by her phone "blowing up" with calls and text messages as the incident unfolded.

Gurpreet described the chaos on the street in front of the Temple as residents stopped traffic on one Oak Creek's busiest streets. Law enforcement descended on the scene with eventually more than 400 public safety officers staking out a position at the Temple and in the Classic Lanes parking lot. Temple family members, desperate to find out any information on their relatives and friends, attempted to get closer to the Temple and even with a limited number of police in place, they were being turned away and pushed back which elevated the tension levels and uncertainty even higher.

Asking her about August 5, 2012 clearly brought back some of the memories and images of that day and as we sat together, a close friend sitting at her side for support, she recounted the events, occasionally stopping to control her emotions or to reconsider my questions. She had been at home at the time of the shootings, but her mother, Jasbir Kaur Dulai, was at the Temple that morning, at one point hurriedly darting from the safety of the pantry, where the woman had fled when the shooting had started, to shut off the burners on the stove.

As Wade Michael Page fired on her mother and another woman from the Temple, the bullets shattered the granite wall at the rear of the kitchen, causing fragments to spray across the kitchen floor, the shrapnel cutting her feet as she ran back to the pantry. At that moment, Page had missed his targets, his attention perhaps diverted by the arrival of the police outside. Telling me the story of her mother and that brush with the killer of her community members and the leader of her Temple, she paused to reflect on how close she had come to losing her mother on that day. The pain of that recollection clearly affected her willingness to understand how other members of her community have suffered since then.

The night before, on Saturday, August 4, Gurpreet had been celebrating *Teeyan* with her friends and family, a *Punjabi* summer festival where women gather together to dance and enjoy each other's company. She had been out late that evening, her mother graciously allowed her to sleep late, a decision which may have saved her life. Waking on Sunday morning as her phone alerted her to the situation at the Temple, she quickly dressed in a panic, a friend picking her up and driving to the Temple shortly after 10:00 a.m. She noticed nearby residents on the street stopping traffic and she immediately tried to assess the situation, knowing from her phone that multiple people had been shot inside the Temple, but at that point unable to determine if her mother was alive or dead.

As a Temple member who spoke *Punjabi*, she was immediately pressed into service as an interpreter by the first-responding law enforcement agencies. They were desperately trying to determine what had happened inside the Temple, unable to effectively communicate with the other members who had rushed out of the Temple and run across Howell Avenue. She served in that role for most of the rest of that day describing the scene as "chaotic, uncontrolled and tense," with little official information available until much later in the day. The lack of interpreters contributed to the agitation felt by the family members and combined with a delay in identifying the victims, added to a growing sense of dread.

In the early afternoon Gurpreet was finally reunited with her father and mother; each of them had been in a different place that morning, but now they were working together in the makeshift relief center. They tried to calm the members, assisted the police, and helped in any way they could. Her father had been working at his gas station that morning, and as one of the leaders of the Temple, he played an important role that day in communications between law enforcement and the Temple community.

As the hours passed and the questions about the identity of the victims grew, Gurpreet spent much of the day consoling the growing number of Sikhs who had assembled inside Classic Lanes. Several families were unable to verify the whereabouts of their family members inside the Temple. Despite a significant presence of law enforcement inside the building, getting any reliable information was difficult. Gurpreet focused on feeding the people there, making sure they were comfortable in the large basement hall, away from the media who had assembled outside.

Gurpreet's father Balhair Dulai had taken a different path

to the United States. Raised in England, he had come to Oak Creek more than 35 years earlier and had established several businesses while he raised his family in America, firmly holding on to his Sikh faith. He played a significant role as a liaison with our leadership team during the aftermath of the shooting in the first week, and his knowledge and understanding of the Sikh community was vital in our ability to work with them.

Notifications came slowly but as they did the grief and sorrow of that day spread like waves through the building, each family slowly confronting the reality that they had already begun to know hours earlier. Unable to contact their loved one or to find anyone who had seen them alive, many families only hope had been that perhaps somehow their family member had just been injured and had been taken to a nearby hospital. Around midnight, the full extent of the tragedy was beginning to be known. Six members of the Temple had been killed with several injured, one of them critically. The shooter was dead, but that reality had no impact on the families who had been waiting at Classic Lanes.

It was late in the evening Sunday night when Gurpreet finally returned home after a day filled with horror, waiting, grieving, and finally, certainty and incredible sadness.

On Monday, less than 24 hours after the shooting and with just a few hours of sleep, Gurpreet drove the elder women of the Temple around in a van. They visited the homes of each of the families who had suffered a loss, comforted each other, and talked about the lives of the victims, cut short by violence.

For a young woman driven by her faith and given significant responsibility in the hours and days after the shooting, she had helped her community in any way she could. She provided an example to the other youth of the Temple and inspired them to do more, and to serve others. They would continue to do this beyond their own Temple. In the months that followed, they would help out at other events in the community and participate at interfaith gatherings designed to break down the barriers between different cultures and faiths.

Despite all that had happened and everything she had been a part of from the very first moments after the shooting through the months of grieving and healing after, Gurpreet remained focused on her family, Temple community, and education. When I asked her about the future, and whether or not she has an optimistic view of our country and the larger issues of violence, hate crime, and the respect and acceptance of different faiths, she responded with a hesitant "I hope so." We talked about her friends, many who are not Sikh, who had helped her both on the day of the shooting and in the preparations for the vigil. They had cut out headscarves from large swaths of fabric and constructed the flags in a makeshift assembly line set up at City Hall the day after the shooting.

As I've said many times since August 5, I have significantly more faith in the youth of our country to do the right thing than I do with their parents. While reports of bullying and mistreatment of minorities are certainly are on the rise, I believe that young people today are more open and willing to accepting those who are different. Skin color seems to be less of a roadblock to conversation and friendship than it used to be. In Oak Creek, the demonstration of togetherness and compassion by our students clearly was one indication that they understood they had a role to play. Their willingness to accept different cultures and to embrace the diversity among us brings some hope for the future, not just for Sikhs, but for all of us. Gurpreet, who has lived her entire life in Oak Creek, understands her role in that future as she mentors the youth of the Temple, completes her education, and moves on to the next part of her life.

Billings, Montana — *Not in Our Town*

Patrice O'Neill and the *Not in our Town* producers came to Oak Creek shortly after the Sikh Temple shooting. They asked to interview Chief Edwards and me for what would eventually turn out to be part of the documentary *Waking in Oak Creek*. It told the story of our police response and the actions of the community after August 5, highlighting several of the victims' family members as they coped with the aftermath of the shooting. We spent hours with their camera crews talking about specific events related to the shooting, but also the larger issues of hate crime, community-based policing, and the engagement of local faith groups in our community response.

Much of what we had done after the shooting was based on our relationship with the members of the Sikh Temple of Wisconsin. They had worked with us to build trust, communicated their concerns, but more importantly reached out to other groups in the community. Because of the outreach done by the Temple leadership, the victims' families, and particularly the youth group of the Temple, the broader community began to understand that they were no different from them. Connections were quickly established across lines of religion, race, and culture, and took what had been a motivation for a hate crime and turned it into a lasting bridge to a safer, more diverse community.

When the documentary *Waking in Oak Creek* was
completed and premiered in Oak Creek in March 2013, it
was clear that we now had the opportunity to participate
in a national discussion on community policing and
response to hate crimes. The U.S Department of Justice's
Community Oriented Policing Services program and NIOT's
O'Neill had asked us to organize a NIOT Gold Star City
committee to implement a community wide effort to
participate in the Gold Star charter city program. Bringing
law enforcement, faith, arts and media, civic and school
leadership together, it was part of a national effort to build
a model for anti-hate initiatives by telling the stories of
communities who had found positive solutions to respond
to hate.

There were earlier examples for us to follow. In 1993,
residents of Billings, Montana were faced with a growing
number of crimes directed at minority families and
institutions. White supremacist groups had placed hate-
filled flyers on the windshields of vehicles in town. A
Jewish cemetery was desecrated and a local family's
window was broken by a brick, thrown into the bedroom
of a six year old boy.

As the local media began to report the stories, local
activists, faith and city leaders, and the chief of police
asked the community to respond. Businesses and city
leaders sponsored marches, vigils, and a local painters

union volunteered to paint over hate-filled graffiti in an overwhelming community response to acts of hate. A local newspaper ran a full-page image of a menorah and almost 10,000 residents and businesses put them up in their windows. Eventually the incidents subsided and Billings was seen as a model for community response. These events inspired the first of many NIOT documentaries aimed at telling the stories of communities and individuals that stood up to hate.

Twenty years after that first NIOT documentary was produced on the Billings movement, we were invited to attend the NIOT National Leadership Gathering in June 2014. Pardeep and Kanwar Kaleka, Kamal Saini, reformed skinhead Arno Michaelis, Murphy and I were part of the opening night screening and panel at the Northern Hotel in Billings. Most of us had never been to Montana and as Murphy and I arrived at the airport in Billings, it was clear that the event was important to the community. A large banner for the Gathering hung in the concourse and at the hotel downtown. Over the next three days, the schedule of events included screenings, panels, breakout sessions, and workshops centered on the Gold Star program and the strategy to build safer and more inclusive communities. Steve Bullock, Governor of Montana, made the opening remarks for the Gathering and *Waking in Oak Creek* was the featured film on Friday night.

As we watched the film along with hundreds of other attendees from communities across the country, it was quiet in the room. The significance of the shooting and the story of the Temple victims and their families were deeply felt by the audience and as the film ended, many in the crowd wiped tears from their faces. For the next hour we answered questions on the shooting, touching on what the Temple families' experiences had been, to what made our response to the shooting different. Murphy was asked about his injuries and the sequence of events as he arrived at the Temple that day. Near the end of the discussion, Kamal talked about the lessons of August 5 and the words that guided him as he dealt with the loss of his mother Paramjit Kaur. He used a quote from Dr. Martin Luther King to make a larger point. "Darkness cannot drive out darkness, only light can do that. Hate cannot drive out hate, only love can do that," Kamal said.

Over the next few days, we met many of the leaders and NIOT representatives from the other communities. We shared stories and listened to their personal accounts of hate crimes and intolerance they had witnessed. Saturday night, at the Babcock Theater in downtown Billings, a screening of the original NIOT film about Billings was shown for the public and the conference attendees. After the film, a group of community leaders who had been active in the response to the incidents in the 1990s talked about their roles and the impact it had in Billings then, and in their lives since. While most talked about the successes they had achieved then, others mentioned current concerns related to LGBT rights in Billings and struggles for minority populations in Montana.

In the week before the NIOT National Gathering, the Billings City Council debated a non-discrimination ordinance for LGBT residents, designed to protect them from discrimination in housing and employment. It was clear that even in Billings, 20 years after they set an example for the rest of the country on how a community should response to acts of hate, issues remained. To their credit, many of the Billings NIOT members were actively working to see that those individual's rights were protected as well.

As I boarded the plane back to Milwaukee, I was optimistic that the message of Oak Creek was one that could also resonate across the country. Although we were only a city of 35,000 residents, we had demonstrated that by working together and involving our community in the response to an act of violence, we could create an environment that would welcome diversity. The National Gathering had encouraged me to work harder and seek out opportunities for a larger national discussion, one that could truly reduce the number of incidents of violence and hate in our country. I welcomed that opportunity.

Pardeep & Arno — An Unlikely Alliance

*"Seven people died in Oak Creek...,
because untreated suffering was inflamed
by fear, ignorance, and hatred."*
                              ~ Arno Michaelis

In October of 2012, over a cup of tea at a restaurant in
Milwaukee, Arno Michaelis, a former skinhead and white
supremacist, and Pardeep Kaleka, eldest son of Satwant
Singh Kaleka, talked about their lives. Each had arrived
there on a much different path. Michaelis early in his life
was full of hatred and anger and was a founding member
of one of the largest white supremacist organizations in
the world. A simple act of kindness and his role as a single
parent caused him to reevaluate his life. For Pardeep, the
decision to call and meet Michaelis was based on a
question. *Why would someone who used to be like Arno
have wanted to kill his father?*

Three months earlier another white supremacist, Wade
Michael Page, had brutally killed his father at the Sikh
Temple of Wisconsin. Pardeep had heard about Michaelis
through his work with the group *Life After Hate*, and the
book that Michaelis had written based on his experiences.
His transformation away from a life consumed with hate to
one of compassion was not the typical storyline for a
young man who spent his teenage years as an alcoholic

201

and the lead singer of a hate-metal band called the
Centurions. For Pardeep, a former police officer and a
teacher, the conversation not only helped him understand
people like Page, but also pushed his teaching in a
different direction. Their first four-hour meeting
eventually brought the two together as friends and allies
in the war against hate.

I had met Pardeep just a day after the shooting, Arno a
few weeks after that. In the months after the shooting our
paths crossed many times. At forums in the community
and at the Temple services, I felt like I had also become
part of the extended family of the Temple. As Pardeep and
Michaelis developed a bond, their willingness to take their
experiences and create a teaching curriculum and service
organization around them resulted in the founding of
Serve2Unite. Along with his brother Amardeep Kaleka and
other members of the Temple community, Pardeep's
group taught children to be *peacemaker*s, and encouraged
them to create service projects to advance the concepts of
diversity, collaboration, and engagement. Through
workshops, assemblies, and mentorships, the two worked
at inner city schools in Milwaukee and the suburbs to
spread their message of compassion.

The example was clear; the pairing significant and
powerful. If these two men, one a former skinhead, the
other a Sikh whose father had just been killed by a white

supremacist, could get along, then clearly there was hope for anyone.

Michaelis had helped me out at several events in the months and year after the shooting, including a community forum on violence that the City of Oak Creek and our school district hosted in the spring of 2013. Michaelis was in the audience and at one point addressed the crowd. He told his personal story and talked about the kindness of a stranger, who helped him at a time when he desperately needed it. This simple act had flipped a switch for him in his life, and moved him away from a life of hate. Michaelis has a very low, baritone voice, scratchy from his days as a singer with the band, and the distinctive tone of his voice has captured the attention of any audience I've ever seen him speak in front of.

Pardeep is a family man, and through his friendship, I met his brother, his many cousins, and wonderful mother Satpal Kaleka. She anchored the family in the aftermath of the shooting, despite the tremendous grief she felt after her husband's tragic death. She hid in the pantry with the other women and children who had been in the *langar* hall and the kitchen that morning as Page began his rampage. A split-second decision that undoubtedly saved their lives.

When I've appeared with Pardeep and Michaelis at events in Oak Creek and Milwaukee, it's readily apparent that the two have made the conscious decision to devote their lives to their work, often speaking for free at schools in the area, or other public events. With young children at home, it can't be easy for Pardeep or Michaelis to take the time away from their families, and it certainly would have been easier to let others speak out on the issues. But the power of their joint message in the context of their histories is one of the most inspiring things I've ever witnessed.

In the film *Waking in Oak Creek,* I talk about the wisdom of youth and my hope that young people can lead us out of the mess we are in when it comes to issues of race and acceptance of other cultures and lifestyles. It's easy to point to guns as the source of the problem when it comes to violence in our country. Whether or not a gun is available to a person with a hate-filled agenda and the intent to act, the principle motivations are still anger, rage, and hate. As he works in the schools, Michaelis speaks to that issue and the need to interject education and compassion into understanding the drivers of violence. His experiences give him credibility in the classroom. His voice carries the message of his experiences and his own personal conversion.

Young people in the United States now live in a country with tremendous diversity and the opportunity to grow up and interact with other children who look different than they do. They share personal stories unlike their own, from countries and cultures scattered around the world. As Pardeep, Michaelis, and *Serve2Unite* expand their efforts in education, teaching the values of accepting and appreciating the differences between us, the children they teach offer us the best chance for a long-term solution to the problems of hate and the violence it creates.

Back to the White House

In November of 2014 I returned to Washington D.C., my third trip to the nation's capital since the shooting at the Sikh Temple of Wisconsin. On a cold, rainy weekend that coincided with my fifty-sixth birthday I was scheduled to visit the White House Office of Intergovernmental Affairs on Friday, and attend the SALDEF National Gala on Saturday night, the same event I had attended in October of 2012, just after the shooting. Jasjit Singh, the executive director of SALDEF, had invited me to attend this year's event, and I was delighted to be asked back.

Elias Alcantara and Rohan Patel, who both worked in the Office of Intergovernmental Affairs in the White House, had also invited me to meet with them on my trip. I had come to know each of them from my work on several initiatives with the Vice President over the last two years, including his Google + hangout on gun violence in April of 2013. They asked if I would be interested in signing on to the President's *My Brother's Keeper* initiative, which he had launched in February of 2014. It was a program designed to improve the lives of young people across the country, particularly those of color. I felt in our own way Oak Creek could play a role in delivering a better quality of life to our youth, even though we didn't face many of the problems in Oak Creek that minority children faced in the larger cities around the country.

Since the first few days after the shooting in Oak Creek, I had taken an interest in helping out Gurvinder Singh, the young Sikh from the Temple who had lost his father in the attack. We had become friends, and as recently as a week before my White House visit he had asked for my help in finding a job in Oak Creek. I had met with him at a local McDonald's restaurant during the summer and he talked about his family and what he wanted to do in the future. He was very interested in music, and told me he had recorded some *Punjabi* songs and posted them on his Facebook page. He was a talented young man, and if I could use whatever influence I had to help him out, it seemed like an easy and right thing to do. I was inspired by the young people at the Temple. They understood their own story's significance in the greater context of race and religious diversity in the U.S. and actively worked to educate and tell their story to their peers and to the other residents in the community.

As I passed through the first level of security for the White House at the corner of 17th Street and State Place, I noticed that the access to the White House complex had changed since my last visit. Several recent incidents with fence-jumpers, including one person who had actually made it inside the White House with a weapon, had ramped up the attention of the Secret Service. This led to the recent resignation of Julia Pierson, who had served as Director of the Secret Service under President Obama. On

my previous visits after showing my identification and
being let inside the gates, I could take an immediate left
up the stairs to the West Wing. On this visit, I was greeted
inside the gates by a White House intern, who then
escorted me into the building. As we waited in a small
reception area on the first floor, I noticed the pictures that
adorned the walls of almost every hallway and office in the
building. Captured moments from recent events and some
going back decades earlier told the story of the Presidents
and their interactions with the public and other heads of
state. If there was a benefit to being invited to the White
House, for me it was the opportunity to be able to see
these images and the other mementos of presidential life
in the White House.

After a few minutes, Rohan Patel, Special Assistant to the
President and Deputy Secretary of the Office of
Intergovernmental Affairs met us, and we rode a small
elevator up to the fourth floor of the White House. I had
brought several copies of *Waking in Oak Creek* with me on
this visit; one each for the President, the Vice President,
and for their staff to watch. I also included a personal
letter with the copies of the DVD, thanking them for their
service to the country and for their willingness to engage
with Oak Creek, both on the events of August 5, 2012, and
on larger issues. I had met Patel on a previous visit, and we
shared stories of our families and I filled him in on my
work with the Sikh community in Oak Creek and with the

national Sikh organizations. My bond with the Sikh community had only gotten stronger in the recent months and this trip highlighted that point. The film told the story of what happened and how that event changed the lives of everyone involved. The real story was what happened after the shooting, in the relationships that were established, and the work that was being done to educate the public on the real contributions of the Sikh community. Their version of the American story of immigration and struggle for acceptance in a new country was one they wanted desperately to tell.

We sat in a meeting room adjacent to a suite of small offices where many of the White House interns worked, right alongside staff and in very tight, cramped quarters, their desks just feet away from each other. Given the age of the White House it wasn't surprising to see that space was an issue, particularly given the many duties of the people working in the building. I would imagine that it was a young person's dream job to work in the White House, and the interns that I had met told me as much, relating their stories and backgrounds on every visit I took to the White House.

A little later, Elias Alcantara, Associate Director of the Office of Intergovernmental Affairs, joined us. I knew Alcantara fairly well as we had talked on the phone numerous times in the last two years. Always friendly and quick to ask how Oak Creek was doing, he had been an intern himself, joining the White House staff in 2012. Patel had mentioned earlier on a White House conference call on the MBK program that "Elias was a rising star" in the White House, and he noted that Alcantara had been recently named to the *40 under 40 list of Latino Voices* by the Huffington Post.

Meeting with two staff members of the Office of Intergovernmental Affairs was an opportunity that mayors of smaller communities typically don't get, and I used the time to highlight what we had done in Oak Creek after the shooting. Patel and Alcantara accepted the DVDs of *Waking in Oak Creek*, and even pitched the idea of a White House screening at some date in the future. I eagerly accepted that offer and later that evening texted the producer of the film, Patrice O'Neill, with the news.

I had shared a few chapters of this book, still a work in progress, with Alcantara a few weeks earlier, and he commented on several of the mentions related to the White House and the President. The story of what happened at the Temple had obviously connected Oak Creek to Washington D.C. and that link is one that continues to this day. The Office of Intergovernmental Affairs recognized and nurtured that relationship.

It was a very busy day at the White House and already late

in the afternoon on a Friday, so the meeting didn't last more than 45 minutes. On my way out, Alcantara showed me where Vice President Biden worked when he was in the building. It was also a very small office that didn't look any different from any of the others we passed. He mentioned that Irene Hsu, who had called me on the day of the shooting to let me know that the President would eventually be reaching out to me, had her office on the same floor.

Alcantara walked me down the driveway on the north side of the White House, past the row of television network tents where the correspondents covering the White House did their nightly news stand-ups. It was still raining lightly, and as we shook hands, he wished me a happy birthday. I would be celebrating it the next day with Sikhs from around the U.S. and in many ways it was a perfect way to celebrate it. What had happened in Oak Creek had connected me not only to the Sikh community but also to Washington D.C. From a horrible day in early August of 2012, to several trips to the White House in the two years after, the opportunity to tell the story, to educate the public on what Sikhs were really about, and how their story mirrored other immigrant stories, including those of my own grandparents, was a powerful one. Instead of catching a taxi at the corner, I turned south and walked along the west gates of the White House complex to the South Lawn area, full of tourists taking pictures, contorting their heads through the iron gates to get a better view of the White House.

I walked all the way to the National Mall before I finally hailed a taxi and made it back to my hotel, appropriately named The George after the first President. More than two years had passed since the shooting at the Temple. In that time I had been given access to the White House, asked to speak about Oak Creek and the events of August 5, 2012 in many other venues, and built new relationships that gave me a forum to talk about the significance of what happened well beyond the borders of Oak Creek.

As it did on each previous visit, the White House had renewed my spirit and gave me the encouragement to push harder on the issues that the shooting raised. Much of what had happened to me since then was not the result of that act of violence, but in the response to it. I was encouraged by what I saw in Oak Creek and other cities around the country. Could our story be a rallying point for a sea change in how we relate to each other as individuals? If the shooter had intended to drive a wedge between cultures and races, could the ultimate irony be that what actually happened was the beginning of a dialogue that changed that dynamic in the opposite direction?

SALDEF — Two Years Later

The Smithsonian's National Portrait Gallery sits at the
intersection of 8th and F Streets in downtown
Washington, D.C. Like many other notable public buildings
in the capital, its exterior is sandstone and marble and
inside are the portraits of nearly every American
President. In the afternoon before the SALDEF gala I
walked from room to room in the Hall of Presidents,
occasionally stopping in front of a painting to consider it
more closely, taking in the span of 200 plus years of
leadership in a couple of hours. I had plenty of time before
the night's festivities kicked off at the Grand Hyatt hotel,
and spending some time among the presidents certainly
gave me the opportunity to consider the enormity of the
issues each of these leaders had to wrestle with during
their terms.

The significance of these presidential portraits on my visit
to Washington was wrapped up in the concept of
leadership and the role it plays in the actions of those of us
who serve in that capacity. Certainly, my role as mayor
was not even in the realm of consequence or significance
of what a president deals with everyday, but the issues we
faced in Oak Creek as a result of the shooting at the Sikh
Temple of Wisconsin did have national implications. How
we live together, how we relate to each other, and in the
harsh reality of August 5, 2012, our failure to accept each

other, were problems we have to face head-on. Washington, Lincoln, and Franklin Roosevelt each tackled enormous challenges during their tenures as president. But each understood that facing up to these challenges was not a rhetorical question but one that required a solution. If I had learned anything in the two years since the shooting, it was that I felt an obligation to work towards improving not only the acceptance of the Sikhs in my own community, but challenging the notion that new Americans were somehow different than those who had been here before.

The National Portrait Gallery is a quiet place, each room filled with a mix of portraits and sculpture. Many of the portraits are very large, some offering life-size depictions of the subjects, giving the viewer the opportunity to look directly into the eyes of historic public leaders. As it had on my previous visits, the time I spent there added context to my trip. It wasn't just about the Presidents' stories, but in the events they led the country through. The founding of a nation, the Civil War, the Great Depression, each required a willingness to step outside of what was comfortable or accepted, and take on popular opinion. As I walked down the steps out of the building that day, I felt a renewed excitement to challenge the status quo on the subjects of race and tolerance in the county, regardless of the popularity of that choice.

The SALDEF National Gala is held every October in Washington, D.C. and is a celebration of each year's activities in the organization's effort to promote and protect the rights of Sikh Americans to enjoy the same freedoms as every other American. It is not a solemn event. Music, inspiring speeches and calls to action are all important parts of the gathering, but the conversations held at tables, and in the hotel before and after is something that I will always remember.

As I arrived, I ran into Jasjit Singh, Executive Director of SALDEF, who had invited me back to this year's event. When he had asked me to come to the gala a few months earlier I had let him know that it was my birthday on the same night, so he wished me a happy birthday as I came down the escalator of the Grand Hyatt to the reception hall. Jasjit had been one of the first Sikh leaders in Oak Creek shortly after the shooting, and his wisdom and guidance helped me understand some of the sensitivities of the Sikh community early on. I was one of the first guests to arrive, a habit I've had for years, never wanting to be late for anything important. Entering the VIP reception room, an older Sikh gentleman waved me over to his table. As I greeted him and we exchanged business cards, I realized it was the guest of honor for the event that night.

Dr. Narinder Singh Kapany was considered to be the

"Father of Fiber Optics" and was being honored with the Bagat Singh Thind award for his work on behalf of the Sikh community. He founded the company Optics Technology and holds over one hundred patents related to fiber optics technology, in addition to having taught at Stanford University. As I handed over my business card I felt a little inferior given his significant resume, but as we talked he asked about my role in Oak Creek and what I had done in the response to the shooting. He is in his eighties, but his enthusiasm and humor were those of a much younger man, perhaps a byproduct of his years spent as an educator of young people. He introduced me to several of his friends who had come from all over the country to see him presented with the award, many of whom were also very distinguished in their careers.

For the gala, I was seated at the same table as the members of SALDEF's leadership team, some who I had met previously at the 2012 gala when I was asked to speak about the shooting at the Sikh Temple. That was just two months after the shooting when I was still getting my public speaking legs, and wrote out most of my speeches word for word. I rarely do that now, typically just writing down some key words or phrases I want to highlight. As in most things, the more often you do it the easier it gets, and that certainly was true when it came to talking about the details of August 5, 2012. Although the emotion of that day never lessens.

I was surprised how many of people at the gala I had met
before, either in Washington, on a visit to Oak Creek or at
the Sikh Temple. It wasn't unusual to get a call on my city
cell phone from someone coming in from out of town who
wanted to stop and say hi, or ask me to meet with them at
the Temple. Part of my role was as an ambassador to the
city, and if that meant showing them where the tragedy
happened, I was certainly happy to oblige. I've met
hundreds if not thousands of Sikhs and I can honestly say
I've never been met with anything other than respect and
appreciation from all of them.

One of the amazing coincidences of the evening happened
during one of the award presentations. Peterson Milla
Hooks, an advertising agency in Minneapolis had worked
with GAP, the apparel company, to produce an ad
featuring a Sikh American actor named Waris Ahluwalia.
The ad was part of an effort to highlight the positive
impact of Sikhs and others who are social activists and
difference-makers in the world. In the ultimate act of
social responsibility, the agency responded to the defacing
of one of these ads in a New York subway with a social
media campaign reaffirming their support of the Sikh
community. They were being honored with the Sikh Image
Award, and Tom Nowak, President of Peterson Milla
Hooks, was accepting the award. As he began to speak, he
mentioned that when the shooting in Oak Creek had
happened he was taken aback, because he was from Oak

217

Creek. As I heard him say those words, I was shocked. When he mentioned that he was an Oak Creek High School graduate, as I was, it was hard to believe I had never been aware of that before that night. After the gala, we had a chance to sit down and talk, and he told me that when he was growing up in Oak Creek my brother Bob had been his basketball coach. It was encouraging to see Oak Creek continue to be connected with positive stories related to the Sikh community and I was proud that like our city, his agency had also done the right thing.

Unlike most banquets or celebrations, dinner at the gala is served after the ceremony, and the food was a wonderful sampling of Indian cuisine, with varying degrees of spice in the different entrees. It was served buffet style and as I waited in line I met even more attendees who wanted to share their stories with me and ask how Oak Creek was doing. It was remarkable that just like our own Sikh community members, their overriding concern always seemed to be how the rest of us were getting along.

It was the perfect way to spend my fifty-sixth birthday, with my extended Sikh family in a city that celebrates diversity and achievement. I left the celebration feeling connected to them in a powerful new way. They understood, like I did, that the solution to the problems of race and religious intolerance in our country lies in the understanding that all of us are Americans. The Sikhs were

an American story as well. Each the same, but with our
own unique twist on how we got here.

A Way Forward

Having lived through the aftermath of the events of August 5, 2012, it was not hard to look back on what happened that day in Oak Creek and think about how much, and how little, had changed. When tragedy strikes any community, it can certainly define the perception and forever link that place to the incident. Many cities across the country, too many, have witnessed the horror of a mass shooting and joined the long list of cities where people have been killed without motive or apparent reason. In Oak Creek we could have accepted that fate, quietly moved on, and hoped that the media would just go away and life would return to normal.

For our community, still in shock in those first few days after the shooting, it was beyond belief that a gunman could walk into a place of worship in Oak Creek and brutally murder six people. The manner in which it happened, the savagery of the killings, and the merciless attack upon our officer, Murphy, was startling. When faced with the overwhelming grief and sadness of the shooting at the Sikh Temple of Wisconsin, our community came together, many of us willing to stand up and say we would not let the tragedy be the only story. Just 48 hours after the shooting, thousands of our residents and visitors from around Wisconsin and the rest of the country came to a small park in the center of the city and quietly listened to family members talk about the lives of each of the victims. As their personal stories were read to the crowd, we learned that the members of the Sikh Temple were also our neighbors, business owners, and most importantly, part of our community.

Whenever a mass shooting happens in this country the national media are quick to descend on the scene, following familiar patterns of news coverage that typically last only for a few days. Once the interview opportunities are exhausted and the details are well known, that kind of attention usually goes away and the reporters move on to the next story. That was the generally the case here, although during the first two weeks after the shooting both Chief Edwards and I were doing local interviews for radio and television almost nonstop. We realized early on that keeping the media informed was important in a number of ways. Given the nature of the shooting and the fact that it happened in a place of worship, it was key to reassure our residents that the gunman acted alone, and the active threat had ended. But the critical decision, to engage and encourage a relationship with the local media, provided benefits not only in our ability to disseminate information quickly but also to provide transparency, something that is critical in modern day policing and in the public sector. It's very apparent when municipalities take the opposite approach, and our goal from the first day was to develop a good working relationship with the media.

After August 5, 2012, I was often asked to speak on the subject of the shooting and its impact on the city of Oak Creek, the residents, and the temple community. Early on, my comments were largely defined by those six minutes of time from Murphy's arrival to the moment when Page put the handgun to his head and ended what could have been an even more horrific event. The actions of our highly trained and experienced officers contained Page's rampage, and more than likely saved many lives. Page's death put an end point on the shooting, a benefit other cities that suffered similar tragedies did not receive. As of this writing, the suspect in the Aurora, Colorado theater shooting still has not been sentenced, more than two years after the shooting.

The first time I spoke outside of Oak Creek was at a Milwaukee area church on August 20, 2012, as part of a healing service for the victims and the community. I echoed the phrase I had used at the Tuesday evening vigil just two days after the shooting. "We will not let this tragic event define us as a city" and those words carried significance beyond Oak Creek. As I've done every time since then, I closed by asking the audience to join me in an effort to find ways to reduce these tragedies from happening in the future.

Other leaders stepped up and mentored me in the first few days after the shooting, many who called and offered

their support and help. Aurora, Colorado Mayor Steve
Hogan was critical in the formation of my response
strategies in the first week, and his direct experience was
relatable and extremely helpful. Mayor Hogan set the
course for my early conversations with the media,
residents, and our staff, walking me through not only what
I would experience in the aftermath of the shooting, but
also how he personally dealt with it. His willingness to
share his wisdom and guidance is something that I think is
an important lesson for leaders. Mentoring is certainly
nothing new, but mentoring in the wake of tragedy and
networking with other leaders who are facing similar
circumstances can be a leadership point going forward.
I've reached out to other leaders since then, and I hope
that my experiences helped them face some of the issues
they've had to deal with.

Establishing defined and effective communication
channels between local leaders and the media was also
one of our key objectives from the very first moments
after the incident. Within law enforcement, many of the
roles are clearly defined as part of local emergency
government planning or by state and federal requirements
for emergency management preparedness. In our case,
the public spokesperson on the first day was a police chief
from a nearby city, Brad Wentlandt, of the Greenfield
Police department. He served as the on-scene PIO allowing
Chief Edwards to focus on his immediate responsibilities,

freeing him up to manage his officers and make critical decisions on the investigation.

For elected officials, there hasn't been a similar push for guidelines on what to do in these types of events, specifically when it comes to media relations. With the expansion of media coverage and the ability of outlets to report almost instantaneously, you don't have to look hard to see how poorly handled communications can impact the story. For the public, a significant early take-away from the first moments of an emergency event is often framed by the reaction of their local leaders. Creating an emergency plan that details the roles for both elected leaders and their communications or public information offices, can help streamline operations during the already tension-filled first minutes and hours after an event. Despite not having an official plan in place, we followed the lead of law enforcement and worked effectively to get the right message out in that critical first week.

Communities should have emergency preparedness plans in place beyond just meeting basic public health and safety concerns. If they don't, they are putting themselves at risk of appearing less than official, or worse, disorganized. This can open the door for misinformation, adding to unnecessary fears and concerns among the public. Getting the right story out, with critical information related to what's happening on the ground or in some cases, asking the public for their help, can aid in the response and investigation. Local media can be an asset to a municipality or a police department and establishing a good relationship with them gives both the opportunity to tell their story. Local media in Milwaukee and Wisconsin were important assets for us in disseminating critical details about the shooting and the investigation, and I would encourage other leaders to nurture those relationships.

At the time of the shooting, I had been in office for just four months. Having worked in the private sector for 28 years before my election, my previous crisis management experience was confined to dealing with unhappy clients and the occasional issue with an employee. But beginning just after eleven in the morning on August 5, 2012, I was thrust into the role of spokesperson for a city reeling from one of the worst acts of violence in our nation's history. Calling up whatever experience I had did help, and I certainly kept my comments brief and to the point whenever I was being interviewed. Knowing what not to say also helped, and I received significant amount of support and letters of encouragement from other mayors around the country who identified with my situation and reached out to offer their assistance and guidance. I've continued to pay that forward, and have reached out to leaders around the country who have been forced to deal with situations like ours.

Building positive and constructive relationships with any outside agencies we worked with was a theme that provided the backbone for our early response. Dealing with difficult situations is never easy, but understanding that taking a stance that embraced open and honest lines of communication certainly paid off in our handling of the shooting. We understood that given the significance of the event, who was targeted, and the fact that we were talking about a hate crime certainly dictated that our actions needed to be up front.

The group most impacted, the members of our Sikh Temple, responded with incredible composure and compassion from the very first moments after the shooting. Young people at the Temple like Gurpreet Dulai, Gurmukh Mangat, and Rahul Dubay mobilized to help the families, serving as interpreters and support for their Temple members, but also showing us what needed to be done and educating the community on the Sikh faith. Elder members from the Temple including Dr. Kulant S. Dhaliwal and Dr. Harcharan Singh Gill helped me understand some of the nuances of life inside the Temple. I followed their examples and without their leadership and guidance my response to the shooting would certainly have been made much more difficult.

In the first few weeks after the shooting, much of my schedule was filled with talking to the media and meeting with the representatives of the Temple families, in addition to performing the regular duties of the job. Grief counselors, national Sikh organizations, and the Department of Justice were on scene within hours and provided resources as quickly as possible. Given the uncertain immigration status of some of the family members, the U.S. Attorney in Milwaukee, James Santelle, spent a significant amount of time and resources sorting through the difficulties of assisting family members trying to get from India to the U.S. to attend the funeral services. Members of our city staff worked tirelessly to coordinate the logistics of each of the events related to the shooting and their willingness to help out were a big part of the reason why the vigil and the funeral services went so smoothly, despite thousands of people in attendance at each event.

It would be impossible to talk about the community response to the shooting without also recognizing that much of the goodwill generated toward Oak Creek was a result of the outstanding police work done on August 5, 2012. Our two heroic officers, Murphy and Lenda, the first responders to the Temple after the flurry of initial dispatch calls came in, put their years of training into use and certainly saved many lives in the process. Murphy, critically wounded just after his arrival, bleeding profusely as he was hauled into the back of a squad car, was able to let the other arriving officers know that he had only seen one shooter, critical information in the chaos of the Temple parking lot crime scene. Lenda, an expert marksman with more than 30 years on the job, made critical tactical decisions when confronting Page that not only resulted in stopping him, but also reduced the likelihood that any others would be hurt, including our own police and fire personnel.

Critical pieces of our response to the shooting were joint decisions between Chief Edwards and myself and were put in place in the first few days. We worked with the City Administrator Jerry Peterson, City Attorney Larry Haskin, and Fire Chief Tom Rosandich as the week developed, coordinating the logistics of holding events as diverse as the community vigil on Tuesday night, the funeral services on Friday, and a visit by the First Lady, all in the span of a few weeks. Hosting a visit from a member of the President's family is a significant event at any time, and adding this to the mix of activities requiring traffic control, parking, and security certainly kept our staff working overtime. The First Lady's visit to Oak Creek High School required coordination between local and federal law enforcement as well as the Secret Service. Located in the center of the city, a wide area around the school was locked down. Despite the concerns associated with it, my meeting with Dr. Dhaliwal and the First Lady went off without a hitch.

Staffing was an issue, particularly for the police department, who early on still had officers on administrative leave, and in Lenda's case, waiting to be cleared by the Milwaukee District Attorney John Chisholm. Since the first few minutes after the shooting, mutual aid calls had directed public safety agencies from around southeastern Wisconsin to respond to the Temple. This assistance was critical because it gave us an expanded workforce to patrol, control access to the crime scene, and to move traffic around that area. In a post-event review, Chief Edwards identified more than 60 agencies involved in the response in the first 12 hours after the shooting. These agencies provided support and resources that we would never have been able keep up with on our own.

There were serious challenges beyond manpower on August 5, 2012, not the least being my inexperience in dealing with emergency situations. While I had just attended an emergency management meeting a couple weeks prior to the shooting, my knowledge of what was required in these types of situations was limited. Given the scope of what had happened at the Temple, an emergency operations center should have been set up. I didn't make that call, but the chiefs and the other department heads had essentially done everything but designate an official room for that use. Many of the roles and responsibilities dictated by the setting up of an EOC fell into place however, based solely on the training that had been done

229

previously.

Controlling the access by the public to the press
conference at the Police Station on Monday, August 6,
2012 was also an area where we had a slight breakdown in
protocol. We should have limited the access to the
courtroom where the press conference was held,
especially given the factors involved in the shooting.
Individuals not directly related to the media or the Sikh
community made it into the room, at one point one of
them asking a question of Chief Edwards. Given what had
happened less than 24 hours earlier, we should have
tightened the security and limited who could enter.

Despite that breakdown, a defining moment of that press
conference was seeing the members of the Sikh Temple,
seated directly in front of the podium, many still in shock
and grieving. At one point one of them came up to the
front of the room and read the name of each victim. I will
never forget that moment, and am convinced that it
signified and demonstrated our willingness to engage with
our Sikh community, even in those first few hours after the
shooting.

Much of the early dialogue between the Sikh Temple and
city leadership contributed to the ongoing success of the
relationship going forward. We have hosted and
collaborated with the Sikh Temple on the Chardi Kala 6K

run-walks, honoring the anniversary and the victims of August 5, 2012 each summer.

Their participation at many community events is now part of our story, their willingness to volunteer or serve continuing one of the most important tenets of their faith, despite all that had happened to them. Balhair Dulai, who stood next to me on the stage at the vigil on Tuesday night, August 7, 2012, now serves proudly on our Community Development Association, bringing his business background and his many years of residency to help us improve our community.

In Oak Creek since August 5, 2012, we have accepted a group of people who were previously silent members of our community. We've embraced their differences while celebrating the diversity they bring to our city. But at the national level, the progress is much slower. When Harpreet Saini testified in front of Congress for the right of Sikhs to be included in FBI crime statistics, he honored his mother and their faith with the right to be recognized, just like everyone else. But for many Sikhs in our country, their right to live without fear is still compromised. They continue to be attacked and linked to acts of terrorism, based solely on appearance and the mistaken belief that they are associated with groups intent on causing harm to the United States or its citizens. The pain of that association has persisted since the first days after the 9/11 attacks on the World Trade Center in New York. Patriotism wrapped up in a warped agenda of revenge against anyone who looks different has resulted in the attacks on members of the Sikh faith and injured or killed many others, including Balbir Singh Sohdi. He was killed just four days after 9/11 while planting flowers outside his gas station in Mesa, Arizona, mistakenly targeted by someone who thought he looked like one of the terrorists who carried out the attack.

Having spent a considerable amount of time in the Sikh community since August 5, 2012, I can attest to their willingness to step up and tell their unique American story, linking it to the stories of many other immigrants who have stepped on our shores.

The story of Oak Creek and our Sikh community demonstrates on a local scale what can happen when people look past their differences to understand the common bonds we all share. Our families, traditions, and sense of community are not unique to one group, race, or religion. If we've done anything in Oak Creek it's to communicate that small cities can show leadership on this issue. Our residents have certainly made the case that it can happen, even in the heart of the country, far away from the big cities and the nation's capital. This is a message I took away from a conversation I had with Vice President Joe Biden, who told me that real change happens in small towns and cities in America, and doesn't need the endorsement of Washington, D.C. to get it done.

One of the challenges we face as a country is addressing how we come to grips with violence, particularly gun violence, as it continues to affect our daily life. It is a subject that dredges up old arguments about gun control and personal freedoms, and as we've seen over our recent history, creates more discussion than it does action. In many conversations and speeches over the past two years, I've often made the point that America is a country of great resources and great minds. Brilliant educators and researchers devote billions of dollars and significant amounts of time to solving the great problems of our age. But we continue to falter when it comes to societal problems and concerns, and in my opinion, the reason lies in our acceptance of politics as the sole arbiter of change. Despite significant public outrage over recent mass shootings, including the horrific slaughter of innocent children at Sandy Hook Elementary in Newtown, Connecticut, we are no closer now to an answer on why these things happen, or how to stop them.

When I received the two phone calls on the morning of August 5, 2012 from Chief Edwards and Chief Rosandich, my life changed as well. From that moment on, I was motivated to help a group of people who were hated and targeted solely because of how they looked. They had been working and praying in the Sikh Temple of Wisconsin that morning, oblivious to any danger outside. When Wade Michael Page arrived at the Temple and began to fire his gun, killing five men, one woman, and injuring three others, he intended to kill. His motivations will probably never be known, but it's clear that he chose his target based on what it represented in his mind, however delusional or misguided that perception was. Whether we can figure out Page's motivations or not, it's our responsibility to seek out solutions to try to prevent this from happening again, regardless of the difficulty of answering that question.

In the spring of 2013, Carl Mueller from Mueller Communications in Milwaukee approached me about an idea he had, based on his feeling that Oak Creek provided an excellent example of how a community should respond to acts of violence. We met to talk about his idea but also to lay the groundwork for what would eventually become Oak Creek Cares, a charitable donor fund under the guidance of the Greater Milwaukee Foundation. Mueller's idea was a simple one: Raise money to fund and support programs that reduced violence and made communities safer and more secure. The idea certainly wasn't new, but it did leverage our success story with an opportunity to look for answers to the problem of violence in our country. Shortly after we signed our agreement in the offices of the Greater Milwaukee Foundation, we received our first donation of $5,000 from Eder Flag Company of Oak Creek, the largest producers of flags and flagpoles in the U.S. That donation launched the Oak Creek Cares Fund and it's my hope that the fund continues to grow and nurture ideas that might eventually find solutions to these terrible acts of violence, which happen too frequently, and often with no apparent motivation.

When I first met with the representatives of the Sikh Temple, just a day after the shooting, in the cafeteria of our local Salvation Army, I had little knowledge of their faith or their history. In the time since, I've come to know them as friends and neighbors and discovered many details about what they believe in and how they fit in to the broader discussion of race and religion in our country.

I was impressed then and I continue to be today with the compassion and the composure they demonstrated to me despite their unbelievable personal tragedy and loss. I promised them that I wouldn't let their story be forgotten, or let those six lives go unnoticed. My story is now part of theirs, and will be for the rest of my life.

On my desk in my office at home sits a black three-ringed binder full of well wishes and condolence letters sent to me after the shooting on August 5, 2012. Page after page of cards and letters from political leaders, religious organizations, and people from many different countries and backgrounds from around the world. They all share a common phrase; *thoughts and prayers*. I used those same words myself in my first public comments on the afternoon of the shooting. It's my hope that we can find solutions to this epidemic of violence. It starts with a willingness to accept that we are all both different and the same, and that those two concepts can, and should, live peacefully together.

Acknowledgements

When I first started to write down my thoughts about what happened in Oak Creek in August of 2012, I never imagined these words would turn into anything more than just a way to express the incredible emotion and sadness I felt after the shooting. But the telling of the story of the tragedy at the Sikh Temple of Wisconsin became a personal therapy session of sorts, spread out over the course of the almost two years I spent writing this book.

Through all of my interactions and conversations over these two years, I learned a lot about what happened that day, but also what it meant to suffer a tragedy — from the recollections of the family members to the impact on our community. I've said it many times since then, but I couldn't be any prouder of how my community came together in the days after the shooting. They continue to make me proud to serve as the mayor of a city that stood up against hate, discrimination, and violence.

As a new mayor, I could have never expected to face the realities of dealing with a mass shooting in my first few months in office without the help of a lot of people, and Oak Creek's response was truly a team effort. From the first moments I arrived on scene, City Attorney Larry Haskin and City Administrator Jerry Peterson were at my side, guiding my decision-making and helping me direct city resources to the right places. City Clerk Catherine Roeske, Director of Community Development and Public Information Officer Doug Seymour, Community Public Health Officer Judith Price, and our IT department led by Caesar Geiger, all stepped up and demonstrated a tremendous work ethic, often volunteering to help with the many events related to the shooting. I appreciate all their efforts and willingness to pitch in, allowing us to respond in the way we did.

Thanks to Dianne Hoffmann and Leslie Flynn for their incredible photographs, some of which I've shared in this book. Many of these pictures have been posted on our social media, city website and in various publications. They have managed to capture the emotion and intensity of what happened here in Oak Creek, and their images help to tell our story.

To my new friends and family from the Sikh Temple of Wisconsin, you inspired me on that very first day, and you continue to do so almost three years later. As I write this, we are coming up on the 3rd anniversary of the shooting, and the spirit of *Chardi Kala* carries on and spreads beyond our borders to cities across this country. I've traveled all over the United States to speak about our response and recovery, and our story resonates as a clear example of how diversity and acceptance of our differences can help to build a fabric of healing and hope. I will continue to work to push that message forward.

Leadership is not a solo venture. Without the tremendous wisdom, training, and experience of Police Chief John Edwards and Fire Chief Tom Rosandich, both co-workers and friends, I would have struggled to understand some of the tactical and other critical decisions related to responding to an event like this. Their leadership and the management of their respective departments was at the highest level.

In the book, I wrote about the incredible mentoring I received from a small group of mayors who could directly relate to what I was going through. To Steve Hogan, Ron

Rordam, and Steven Ponto, thanks for your public service and your willingness to share your knowledge. I've continued to pay it forward with other mayors and leaders around the country as they've had to deal with similar tragedies.

When I talk about the significance of those six minutes on August 5, 2012 in the telling of the story of Oak Creek, I must point to two heroic men who stepped up to save the lives of many others that day. Lt. Brian Murphy and Police Officer Sam Lenda put their own lives at risk, and responded the only way they knew how, with years of training and on-the-job police work backing up their split-second decisions. Their response ended the incident at the Temple, and demonstrated clearly why investing in law enforcement is absolutely critical today, with a need for new funding directed related to training and the utilization of new technologies to make our communities, and our country, safer. To all of our first responding public safety officers, you have my gratitude for a job well done.

As my book began to take shape, I called upon my friend Valarie Kaur to lend her in-depth knowledge of the Sikh community to my project, filling me in on some of the traditions and tenets of the Sikh faith, and guiding some of my descriptions of life in and around the Temple. She continues to lead by example as well, sharing her own personal stories through her work with *Groundswell Movement*, a group she founded.

To my wife Kathy and my two amazing daughters, Katie and Chrissy, thanks for all of the behind-the-scenes support. You showed me the importance of family in this story, and I couldn't have held it all together without you being there with me on this journey.

When it came to assembling all the pieces of my story, I had the great advantage of working with two editors on my book. Andy Tarnoff, publisher and co-founder of OnMilwaukee.com, who covered the shooting for his website, brought a reader's perspective to the structure of the book, and encouraged me to dig deeper on some of the personal stories related to the shooting. My friend and business partner, Chris Behlmer, shaped the look and feel of *Six Minutes in August*, and his considerable experience in publishing and design inspired me to get the story right and to tell it in a way that was easy to read. Thanks to both of you.

I write these words sitting in the same chair I sat in when I received the first calls on the morning of August 5, 2012. It's my hope that we can find a way to reduce the number of mass shootings in this country, and to find that answer before any more innocent lives are lost.

Stephen Scaffidi, Oak Creek, Wisconsin, July 17, 2015

I had covered shootings and I had covered death, but I had never covered anything like what happened on August 5th, 2012. I remember being in a parking lot filled with families and loved ones of those who were hurt or killed and saying to myself, "this is different." And it was; not only that day, but I would learn also in the years that followed as victims refused to let their hurt turn into hate and the community called for real change. As I stood in that lot amid a sea of reporters waiting for the newly minted Mayor to step up to a daunting bank of microphones, I thought this poor guy won't know what hit him. I mean, this is the kind of thing that can cripple even the most seasoned of civil servants. But, this is different. The man introduced as Mayor Scaffidi wasn't just there; he showed up. He stood strong and spoke with sympathy, respect and humility. And that's what he would continue to do in the weeks, months, and years to come. I was proud of the Mayor of Oak Creek that day. I'm even prouder of the man I now call my friend. ~ *Annie Scholz, Marketing Manager*

++

Mayor Stephen Scaffidi provides a vivid account of his experience as a new mayor dealing with the aftermath of a mass shooting in his community. Determined not to let Oak Creek be defined by one person's crime of hate and

ignorance, Mayor Scaffidi led a community response which promoted understanding and appreciation of the Sikh community.
~ *Steven Ponto, Mayor, City of Brookfield, Wisconsin.*

+++

"As a journalist who covered the Sikh Temple shooting, reading Steve's account brings back vivid memories, but also shares insight into the back stories of the victims and first responders who humanized this tragic incident. Oak Creek is a member of a club that no one wants to belong to, but we can all learn lessons from this book about tolerance, healing and crisis communications." ~ *Andy Tarnoff, Publisher and Co-Founder of OnMilwaukee.com.*

+++

"Mayor Scaffidi's book is an important and compelling read for every public official. It provides a minute-by-minute rendering of the events that unfolded on August 5, 2012, when a Sikh house of worship in Oak Creek, Wisconsin, became the site of hate violence. Mayor Scaffidi gives us an understanding of what it was like to be the head of a city grappling with the horror and trauma of gun and hate violence. His book should be a warning sign and a call to action for public and private stakeholders around the nation."
~ *Deepa Iyer, Author, We Too Sing America: South Asian, Arab, Muslim and Sikh Immigrants Shape Our Multiracial Future.*

Photo Credits:

Oak Creek Police Department

Leslie Flynn

Dianne Hoffmann

Stephen Scaffidi

Made in the USA
Lexington, KY
05 September 2015